Praise f

Sara Canaday's *Coaching Essentials for Managers* is the ultimate guide to retaining and engaging your employees. It's packed with valuable information, real-world scenarios, and practical exercises that reinforce learning. Readers will walk away feeling fully prepared to coach and inspire their employees to do their best and most engaged work.

—**Dr. Marshall Goldsmith,** *Thinkers50* #1 Executive Coach and *New York Times* bestselling author of *Triggers*, *Mojo*, and *What Got You Here Won't Get You There*

In *Coaching Essentials for Managers*, Sara Canaday demystifies the coaching process and makes it accessible for any manager who wants to play a significant role in employees' growth and development. She provides a valuable start-to-finish blueprint for effective coaching with strategies that are easy to understand and simple to apply. What's unique about this book is that she doesn't just tell you how to be a successful workplace coach, she shows you exactly what that looks like through case studies and dialogue for a more powerful impact. This book should be required reading for every manager who wants to develop a high-performing team and retain top talent.

—**Keith Ferrazzi,** American entrepreneur, global thought leader, and chairman of Ferrazzi Greenlight

As a content strategist and former business book editor, my aim is to provide learners with skills they can use to make their jobs easier, more manageable, and increasingly rewarding. *Coaching Essentials for Managers* from Sara Canaday does just that! In this book, Sara highlights valuable insights from her experience as a corporate executive and leadership educator that can help managers transform their teams through the power of coaching. The practical tips and helpful scenarios are exceptional resources. I highly recommend this book for anyone interested in improving their coaching skills and increasing their impact.

> —**Susan R. Williams,** senior content manager, business at
> LinkedIn Learning

While companies are scrambling to retain their employees by offering stay-on bonuses and extended benefits, there is one thing leaders can do to give employees what they really want: a chance to learn and progress. Sara Canaday's *Coaching Essentials for Managers* is the handbook for how to accomplish that. This uniquely compelling book provides readers with specific strategies and tools they can use to help inspire their employees to achieve their best and support their professional goals.

> —**Dr. Marcia Reynolds,** author of *Coach the Person, Not the
> Problem* and *The Discomfort Zone*

In *Coaching Essentials for Managers*, Sara provides leadership wisdom that packs a powerful punch. I've always taken pride in helping my employees reach their potential and fulfill their career aspirations, and the strategies in this book have already helped me do just that. Sara has a unique way of transforming leadership principles and theories into actionable strategies, taking the reader from "why" to "how." She also uses authentic examples and vignettes to drive home her key points with real impact. If you're looking for the shortest path to coaching excellence, this book is for you.

—**Jennifer Webb**, director of marketing at Dell Technologies

In a time and world where coaching is the missing link for leadership, culture, and engagement, Sara Canaday delivers the definitive solution in *Coaching Essentials for Managers*. Sara is right on the mark in stating that "coaching is a leadership superpower," and I'd go so far as to say that coaching is *the* leadership superpower. Organizations and leaders have lost their way when it comes to developing and growing their people. Thankfully, Sara offers us a light to help us find our way back as leaders and organizations, and that light comes in the form of *Coaching Essentials for Managers*.

—**Jeff Nischwitz**, chief impact officer at CoreX Legal, speaker, coach, and author of *Snow Globe Leadership: Shaken Not Settled*

As an executive coach, I appreciate the key strategies and principles in Sara's book, *Coaching Essentials for Managers*. I've watched hundreds of leaders shy away from taking a more active approach to coaching because they were intimidated by the process or felt ill-equipped to do it effectively. This resource is what they need. If you are new to coaching or looking to strengthen your coaching skills as a manager, you will find this book enlightening, easy to follow, and full of actionable strategies you can apply immediately.

—**Muriel Maignan Wilkins**, cofounder of Paravis Partners and
podcast host of HBR's *Coaching Real Leaders*

# COACHING
## ESSENTIALS
### FOR MANAGERS

# COACHING
## ESSENTIALS
### FOR MANAGERS

#### THE TOOLS YOU NEED TO IGNITE
#### GREATNESS IN EACH EMPLOYEE

## SARA CANADAY

NEW YORK  CHICAGO  SAN FRANCISCO  ATHENS  LONDON
MADRID  MEXICO CITY  MILAN  NEW DELHI
SINGAPORE  SYDNEY  TORONTO

1 2 3 4 5 6 7 8 9   LCR   27 26 25 24 23 22

ISBN   978-1-264-57358-5
MHID       1-264-57358-8

e-ISBN  978-1-264-57368-4
e-MHID      1-264-57368-5

Design by Mauna Eichner and Lee Fukui

Library of Congress Cataloging-in-Publication Data

Names: Canaday, Sara, author.
Title: Coaching essentials for managers : the tools you need to ignite
  greatness in each employee / Sara Canaday.
Description: New York : McGraw Hill Education, [2023] | Includes
  bibliographical references and index.
Identifiers: LCCN 2022024585 (print) | LCCN 2022024586 (ebook) | ISBN
  9781264573585 (hardback) | ISBN 9781264573684 (ebook)
Subjects: LCSH: Employees--Coaching of. | Personnel management.
Classification: LCC HF5549.5.C53 C454 2023  (print) | LCC HF5549.5.C53
  (ebook) | DDC 658.3/124—dc23/eng/20220826
LC record available at https://lccn.loc.gov/2022024585
LC ebook record available at https://lccn.loc.gov/2022024586

McGraw Hill books are available at special quantity discounts to use as premiums and sales promotions or for use in corporate training programs. To contact a representative, please visit the Contact Us pages at www.mhprofessional.com.

McGraw Hill is committed to making our products accessible to all learners. To learn more about the available support and accommodations we offer, please contact us at accessibility@mheducation.com. We also participate in the Access Text Network (www.accesstext.org), and ATN members may submit requests through ATN.

# Contents

## PART III
# BEYOND THE ESSENTIALS

# Acknowledgments

**I'm immensely grateful** to my friend and developmental editor Susan Priddy for her tireless dedication to making this book come alive. This is the third book I've written with Susan. In traditional fashion, she brought perspective, structure, and flow to my material, which will make this book easy to follow and worth referencing in the years ahead.

On a broader scale, Susan's impact on my work as an author, speaker, and instructor has been enormous. I value her extraordinary commitment to quality as well as her keen ability to embrace and uphold my brand. I count myself ever so fortunate to have her in my corner.

Special thanks and recognition also go to my editor at McGraw Hill, Cheryl Segura. Cheryl has been an encouraging ally throughout the process. She kept me on track and was clearly dedicated to ensuring that my final work was exceptional.

I also want to thank the many leaders I've known and served over the years. Both my colleagues and clients have been an inspiration to me, and I have learned as much from them as they have hopefully learned from me.

Finally, a heartfelt thank you to my dear friends and family. They influenced my decision to write this book and encouraged me every step of the way. I will be forever grateful for their love and support.

# Introduction

**Through the years,** I've had the honor of coaching hundreds of current and emerging leaders around the world. You probably won't find a more passionate champion for this process, and yet I'm still constantly amazed by the results it can generate.

I've seen dedicated professionals completely transform their careers by making relatively small yet targeted adjustments in their behaviors and attitudes through coaching. It changed the trajectory of their own futures, as well as the outlook for their organizations.

With that said, business coaching today is a far cry from what it was even a decade ago. It's a concept that has evolved dramatically over time.

Before starting my own firm in 2005, I spent seven years working as a senior leader in a large corporation. The concept of "leader as coach" had yet to make its way into the leadership landscape. If you were singled out for coaching in that era, the message was clear: You had a performance problem. Something was wrong that needed correcting. Maybe it was unmet objectives or lagging metrics. Whatever it was, the emphasis was more on preventing the continuation of a downward spiral rather than accelerating upward progress.

Today, if you are selected for coaching, it's a sure sign that the company recognizes your potential and wants to invest in helping you achieve it. Being coached is now perceived as a privilege and an opportunity. Talk about a vast change!

Though I was always dedicated to evolving and expanding my impact as a manager, at the time, I didn't have the insight to adopt this modern approach to coaching. I should have recognized that showing a genuine interest in my employees' career aspirations and more actively supporting their progress would have made a world of difference.

Like so many who are in leadership roles, I understood that my primary role as a leader was to set the direction for my team, ensure quality deliverables, and hold people accountable for producing measurable results. Sure, I would provide candid and compassionate feedback when approached by my employees, but there is no telling what kind of impact I could have had if I consistently coached my employees in the more contemporary sense of the word.

With the benefit of hindsight, I'm convinced that coaching is a leadership superpower—and I'm confident you'll feel the same way after reading this book. You'll also have a better understanding of how to coach your teams.

## WHY YOU SHOULD READ THIS BOOK

Because coaching is a crucial part of being a leader, understanding this competency will help you develop the people who report to you so they can take their careers to new heights. You'll also be helping to stock your organization with the very best talent so it can grow and thrive. But

I want you to hit pause on those ideas for just a brief moment and allow yourself to be . . . selfish.

What's in this for *you*?

That's actually a very good question. There is something oddly counterintuitive about focusing every bit of your energy to create a powerful team that runs like a well-oiled machine, while actively preparing your employees to move on. From that perspective, coaching might sound like a self-inflicted wound waiting to happen. *They advance, and I'm stuck here recruiting and hiring and training all over again.*

My response? Yes, but . . .

## Coaching Is a Deeply Rewarding and Meaningful Experience

Leaders who practice and excel at the art of coaching will almost universally tell you that it's the most rewarding part of being a leader.

I've heard this over and over again from thousands of leaders I've worked with through the years. They tell me that coaching stretches them in a uniquely positive way and reconnects them with the reason many of them became leaders in the first place. It gives them a clearly defined purpose that rises above the chaos of fighting fires, making constant pivots, and even struggling through incredible challenges (like a pandemic). Coaching allows them to plant the seeds of success and watch them grow in real time.

Because leaders have to juggle so many roles, they often feel like they're swimming in a pool that's a mile wide and an inch deep. Coaching allows them to finally take a refreshing dive into one area and really make a difference. Instead of directing, they get to position themselves as collaborators. They get to be creative in a way that's completely separate from their usual focus on the organization's products and services. The benefits of that in our current environment cannot be overstated.

Leadership WITHOUT coaching feels like...

Leadership WITH coaching feels like...

## Coaching Can Elevate Your Impact and Influence

Leaders who establish themselves as excellent coaches become the legendary rock stars of their organizations. That's because team members who know their leaders have their backs and genuinely want them to succeed inevitably perform at unprecedented levels. Their loyalty and commitment are off the charts. And, if a team member does leave, other talented individuals are clamoring to take their place and gain the opportunity to be coached by a legendary leader.

The point is, by developing your reputation as a vibrant leader-coach who repeatedly elicits a winning team response, you'll automatically expand your scope of influence and become more valuable to the organization. That gives you an unbeatable competitive advantage to accelerate your own career.

## Coaching Is a Must-Have Skill to Fuel Your Career Success

Leaders who fail to coach in today's competitive business environment often fall behind their peers in terms of career achievements, recognition, and promotability.

For those of you who like the carrot but still need the stick, this one's for you. From a purely self-centered standpoint, you can't afford to consider coaching as an optional "maybe-someday-when-I-have-more-time" activity.

Think about it this way. Your success as a leader is determined by the success of your employees. Given that direct link, how do workers today describe what they actually need to be successful?

Research from the Association for Talent Development (ATD) published in September 2020 showed that 90 percent of companies expect some portion of their managers to coach their employees, and 75 percent expect all of them to do so.[*] Here's why: When managers coach their direct reports, the organizations get a bottom-line bump. So if you want your career as a leader to flourish, coaching is a must-have, expected skill.

An earlier study by the coaching/consulting firm BetterUp confirmed those findings as well. For this study, researchers asked professionals whether they would rather have a 20 percent pay raise or a manager who was invested in helping them find meaning and purpose in their jobs on the way to greater success.

Believe it or not, 80 percent of the respondents picked the supportive manager who would coach them and actively take part in helping

---

[*] Association for Talent Development, 2020, https://www.td.org/press-release/employee-performance-increases-when-managers-coach-direct-reports.

them get ahead. Again, that's 80 percent. So, four out of five would take a manager who supported their progress over cash.

What does that tell us? Employees want to be coached to help them advance in their careers. They desperately want to do meaningful work and feel connected to the purpose of their jobs. When those two conditions are met, they have higher engagement, increased job satisfaction, and elevated productivity.

The message for leaders is clear. Coaching isn't a nice-to-have skill; it's a must-have leadership competency. If you want to create exceptional teams and accelerate your own career success, becoming an effective coach needs to be a top priority.

## Coaching Keeps Companies More Vibrant and Successful

Coaching requires a significant commitment of time and energy by leaders and their team members. Consequently, everyone ends up asking: "Is it worth it?"

In a nutshell: *Absolutely!* Let's take a closer look at the business case for creating a coaching culture within your organization.

If coaching didn't produce concrete advantages, companies wouldn't even bother. But research consistently shows that it's a smart investment. Organizations that make coaching a priority reap the rewards and enjoy enormous bottom-line impact.

According to *Forbes,* the Institute of Coaching discovered a whopping 86 percent of companies that implement coaching cultures report an outstanding return on the time and money they invest in the process. In what ways? The Institute cites increased engagement and motivation, greater accountability, a streamlined path to identify high potentials, more targeted development opportunities, and a clear demonstration of the organization's commitment to professional growth.[*]

All of that adds up to prove that coaching makes good sense from a business perspective. It works, plain and simple. In fact, the Institute's studies show that more than 70 percent of professionals who receive coaching demonstrate better communication skills, stronger relationships, and increased performance. Companies can leverage those improvements for a competitive edge.

As interest in coaching continues to grow, more and more research is being done to quantify its impact. The results? Overwhelmingly positive. Even dating back to 2014, a study highlighted in *The Journal of Positive Psychology* set out to complete a meta-analysis of coaching effects. The scientists tracked significant, positive impact in five areas: performance/skills, well-being, coping, work attitudes, and goal-directed self-regulation.[†]

All of those quantitative benefits stem directly from coaching's targeted effect on the employees. Plus, the "vote of confidence" that comes from coaching makes employees feel a greater connection with the company, as well as its vision and mission. They begin to see a direct line between what they do every day and the company's success. That sense of ownership translates into loyalty, which then improves retention and lowers costs for hiring and training.

---

[*] *Forbes*, 2019, https://www.forbes.com/sites/carleysime/2019/03/28/how-does-coaching-actually-help-leaders/?sh=4f7e57111645; BetterUp, https://f.hubspotusercontent40.net/hubfs/9253440/Asset%20PDFs/Promotions_Assets_White papers/BetterUp-Meaning%26Purpose.pdf; *Harvard Business Review*, 2018, https://hbr.org/2018/11/9-out-of-10-people-are-willing-to-earn-less-money-to-do-more-meaningful-work.

[†] https://www.tandfonline.com/doi/abs/10.1080/17439760.2013.837499.

While that has always been a compelling advantage, it's never been stronger than it is today.

In 2021 and 2022, a mass exodus from the workforce became known as the Great Resignation. The U.S. Bureau of Labor Statistics reported that a record-high 4.3 million US employees quit their jobs in August 2021.

Why? The Covid-19 pandemic shook things up and, for some, reinforced the idea that "life is short." Workers are now demanding better opportunities, more flexibility, roles that bring them greater satisfaction, or a shot at starting their own businesses. If they aren't happy with their current employers, they feel empowered to move on. All they need is an internet connection, and they can theoretically apply for jobs anywhere around the world. The competition for talent is fierce.

This creates a huge problem for companies that are left without enough workers to support their business models. Beyond that, their significant investments in recruiting and development evaporate when people walk out the door.

The good news? Research shows that employees are much more likely to stick around when they are actively being coached and their talent is being developed.

A LinkedIn Learning report from 2020 states that 76 percent of employees describe professional growth and career development as "very important" to them.[*] (A Gallup survey done in the same time frame found that number to be 87 percent for millennials!)[†] But here's

---

[*] LinkedIn Learning, 2020, https://learning.linkedin.com/resources/workplace-learning-report.

[†] https://www.gallup.com/workplace/236438/millennials-jobs-development-opportunities.aspx.

the kicker: 94 percent of employees say they would stay with an organization rather than leaving if the company invested in their professional growth.

No wonder companies believe in coaching! Reams of research prove that coaching is the essential ingredient required for organizations to produce high-performing teams with loyal employees who work together effectively and generate amazing results.

## Coaching Keeps Team Members More Loyal and Engaged

As we saw with the results from the research from both ATD and BetterUp, individuals who are coached are statistically shown to exhibit higher productivity and increased engagement. The cumulative effect? Enhanced drive and performance.

Focused on leadership effectiveness, The Ken Blanchard Companies have promoted coaching to their global clients for many years. Managers there have also thoroughly documented coaching outcomes and client feedback from those who participated in the process. Their findings, quoted in the following list, confirm the personal benefits of professional coaching. Individuals who are coached tend to:

- Establish and take action toward achieving goals

- Become more self-reliant

- Gain more job and life satisfaction

- Contribute more effectively to the team and the organization

- Take greater responsibility and accountability for actions and commitments

- Work more easily and productively with others (boss, direct reports, peers)

- Communicate more effectively*

No doubt about it, coaching is an enormous motivator.

When employees are selected to be coached, they aren't just gaining a chance to improve their professional skills. They also feel like their talent is being recognized and their potential is being respected. They think: *If my leader sees something in me that's worthy of nurturing and growing, I need to step up my game.*

The other interesting thing is coaching allows employees to uncover a real excitement about their work that might have been missing or just fizzled out over time. The one-on-one guidance helps them better play to their strengths, and they end up doing more work they enjoy. In that way, coaching measurably increases their job satisfaction.

So, is coaching worth it? Yes! The business case for coaching is definitive. Companies and leaders who make it a priority will reap the benefits in lasting ways.

## HOW THIS BOOK IS ORGANIZED

As you move forward, you'll discover this book has three distinct parts.

Part I, "The Essentials," provides the foundation for coaching excellence—the fundamentals, framework, skills, and attributes that form the core of this important discipline. Understanding these

---

* The Ken Blanchard Companies, https://coaching.kenblanchard.com/public/Find_Answers/Benefits_of_Coaching/.

components will make you a stronger, more effective leader who is ready to build talent in strategic ways.

Part II, "The Essentials Applied," gives you an opportunity to consider applications for coaching, including real-world challenges and common obstacles you may face. You'll gain valuable insights that help you translate your knowledge of coaching into a powerful leadership advantage.

And finally, Part III, "Beyond the Essentials," includes helpful tips, additional resources, and concrete tools that support your progress toward becoming a highly influential leader who coaches.

Collectively, these sections create a step-by-step guide to achieve coaching success. Everything you need to know. Everything you need to set yourself apart as a world-class coach.

So, what are we waiting for?

My thoughts exactly! Thank you for joining me on this adventure.

Let's get started!

**PART I**

# THE ESSENTIALS

# Coaching Fundamentals

**The first step on** your journey to becoming an extraordinary coach is to understand the basics involved in the process. In this chapter, I share some fundamentals that provide a foundation for everything that follows.

## COACHING DEFINITIONS

To make sure you are fully prepared to be an effective coach, it's important to understand the different phrases involved in this process. Let's start with definitions of some common terms before moving on.

First up is *workplace coaching*. Workplace coaching is a personalized process that inspires employees to take control of their own development in a way that improves their performance now and maximizes their potential for success in the future. It involves a unique relationship between a leader and a subordinate in which they collaborate to:

- Pinpoint personal challenges and opportunities for growth

- Explore possibilities and evaluate problem-solving options

- Develop goals and prioritize actions

- Maintain momentum toward achieving desired results

Fueling personal growth

Solving problems

The purpose of workplace coaching

Maintaining momentum

Developing goals

As you can tell from those collaborative tasks, "leader-coaches" aren't just leaders who deliver meaningful performance reviews. They coach their employees and have a highly specific approach to genuinely develop their team members in a targeted, ongoing way. Throughout this book, both *leader* and *leader-coach* will be used to refer to your ownership of this process as a coach.

To fully understand the concept of coaching, it might help to know what it's *not*. In other words, it is *not* the same thing as managing, training, or mentoring.

> **Managing** requires staying focused on the facts. Things like team goals. Quarterly sales. Monthly expenses. Managers ask, "Is this person producing the results needed?"

> **Training** is about skill-specific learning—helping employees acquire the skills they need to perform their jobs. Leaders who train their employees ask, "Does this person know how to effectively use the latest sales software?"

> **Mentoring** involves high-level support and advice based on the wisdom of previous experience. Mentors ask, "Would this person benefit from hearing how someone else navigated a sticky situation at work?"

> **Coaching** has a wider lane and a more strategic slant. While it likely includes some elements of managing, training, and mentoring rolled into it, the primary goal of coaching is to make other people more successful. A coach might ask, "Does this person know what's getting in the way of their progress?"

## COACHING OUTCOMES

When coaching is done well, it can generate extremely powerful outcomes, including:

- Transforming employees' capacity to produce
- Helping them identify and eliminate any professional roadblocks

- Guiding them to achieve their goals

- Linking their results directly to team and company objectives

- Preparing them for success at the next level

- Supporting their career aspirations

Coaches today approach their team members with a genuine desire to encourage them and help them succeed. As coaches, they make a deliberate shift into a selfless, supportive mindset. And here's the big differentiator: *They focus on the growth and well-being of their employees in a way that unlocks the potential of each individual. Instead of looking at "what needs to be corrected," they look at "what could be."*

The bottom line? Great coaching can have a transformative effect that expands the capacity for people to generate results like almost nothing else can—if it's done right.

## WHAT COACHING IS AND ISN'T

In order to grasp the importance and goals of coaching, let's take a look at what coaching is and what it isn't.

### What Coaching Is

- **Coaching is focused on both short-term and long-term goals.** Put another way, coaching combines today's immediacy for performance improvement with professional development designed to fuel broader career goals in the future.

- **Coaching is a relationship, not an event.** Instead of framing coaching as a calendar commitment every Tuesday, great leaders think of coaching as something that's ongoing and interactive. It's a continuous dialogue based on honesty and trust. When they agree to coach someone, leaders are entering into an extended relationship for sustained support.

- **Coaching can be formal or informal.** Yes, leaders need regularly scheduled, one-on-one meetings with the employees they coach, but the process can be informal, too. You can coach someone during lunch, in the hall after a conference, or even on the elevator right after a meeting. As coaches hone their skills, they can eventually weave coaching into everything they do and apply it in whatever setting they find themselves.

## What Coaching Isn't

- **Coaching isn't about providing all the answers.** Leaders who coach listen and ask questions. They guide employees to find answers on their own. For instance, *managers* might cut to the chase, saying something like: "Here's what you need to do. . . ." *Coaches* start conversations rather than issuing demands. They ask, "What if . . . ?" It's a different approach with a higher probability of igniting curiosity within employees and encouraging them to become strategic problem solvers.

- **Coaching isn't the right solution for every situation.** Coaching requires an investment of time, and there are situations when that just doesn't make sense. Sometimes leaders need to make decisions, give orders, and propel a project forward. It takes some discernment to know when coaching is the right approach—and when it isn't.

## TWO TYPES OF COACHING

Now that we understand what coaching is and isn't, it's time to explore the two types of coaching needed to make the process well-rounded and ensure you maximize your impact: *Performance Coaching* and *Developmental Coaching*.

### Performance Coaching

Performance Coaching involves helping employees become more effective in their current jobs. This might include guiding them to close particular skill gaps or correcting behavior problems. Accountability also plays a key role in this type of coaching. These conversations could be used to clarify expectations and discuss consequences.

Perhaps you have a superstar employee who is suddenly coming in late and neglecting to turn in reports on time. What's really going on there? On the other hand, you might be dealing with a consistently low performer who hasn't responded to warnings or encouragement. What's behind the disconnect?

The other prime example of a Performance Coaching opportunity is the average-level worker who doesn't seem to be leveraging above-average potential. How can you tap into that potential and move this person into the high-potential category?

## Performance Coaching

**Focus:**

Help employees become more effective in their current jobs

**Includes working together to:**

- Close particular skill gaps
- Correct behavior problems
- Hold coachee accountable
- Clarify expectations
- Discuss consequences

## Developmental Coaching

Developmental Coaching is more about helping employees prepare to meet their long-term career goals.

To make a developmental impact, coaches need to really get to know their employees—their strengths, challenges, and career aspirations. Leaders can help these employees define and clarify their goals and then work to ensure they gain the skills and experiences to prepare them for whatever is ahead.

For example, Developmental Coaching might include talking with employees about strategies for managing multiple high-priority projects or giving them opportunities to become more proficient at making presentations to executives. With this type of approach, coaches also might offer to help employees refine some intangible skills that aren't necessarily integral to their current jobs but will be mandatory at the higher-level positions they desire. Perhaps the coach can address some behavior quirks that might be off-putting or engage in role-play to demonstrate how to navigate a politically charged conversation. Today people are resigning at an alarming rate, and the best thing you can do as a coach is to spend time supporting your employees' career aspirations.

It may seem counterintuitive to talk to your employees about their career aspirations, but consider the compelling statistics on Developmental Coaching. According to the Glint Employee Well-Being Report, employees who see good opportunities to learn and grow are 2.9 times more likely to be engaged.[*] Coaching shows that you care about the professional ambitions of your team members and want to support their growth. The irony? Career coaching tends to lead to more engaged and productive employees who want to stay where they are.

In many cases, employees may be seeking new jobs simply because they aren't experiencing a sense of progress with their careers— a top factor in motivating people, according to Teresa Amabile and Steven Kramer, authors of *The Progress Principle*. Coaching for career development demonstrates to employees that you are actively partnering with them to advance within the organization. Nothing else says "progress" quite like that!

From that perspective, having career conversations with your coachees might be one of the best things you can do right now. Besides engendering loyalty, you could possibly keep them from getting caught up in the tsunami of "let's all quit now because it seems like the trendy thing to do."

---

[*] Anne McSilver, "Discover the Secret Advantage for Learning and Employee Engagement," Glint, 2021, https://www.glintinc.com/blog/discover-the-secret-advantage-for-learning-and-employee-engagement/.

So how can leaders approach the topic of Developmental Coaching with more confidence?

In general, redefine your concept of growth and progress. Let go of the notion that successful career coaching ends in a promotion, new position, or bigger paycheck. Everyone views growth in a different way, so take the time to find out what it means to each of the people you coach. Here are some questions you can use to gain insights about their perspectives on this topic:

- "Based on what you've learned about yourself in the past few years, what does it take to make your work feel meaningful for you? What do you need? Anything you don't need?"

- "What kind of work makes you feel like you are operating in your 'zone of genius'—that place where you are excited to work on a project, your skills are aligned with what's needed to reach the goal, and you are so engrossed in the process that you lose track of time?"

- "Are you interested in sharpening your skills or learning some new ones?"

- "Do you see yourself evolving in your current role over the next two years or making a more dramatic change?"

- "Do you have interest in stepping into a leadership role at some point in the future?"

- "Where do you think you could add the most value within the company?"

- "If you could paint a picture of what you'd love your career to look like in one year, what would we see on the canvas?"

Remember that we can get creative to find solutions that qualify as "growth" for our employees. That doesn't necessarily mean they will pack up their offices and move to another floor or another company. It very well might translate into growth that allows them to take on more responsibility right where they are.

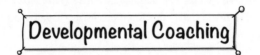

## Developmental Coaching

### Focus:

Help employees prepare to meet their long-term career goals

### Includes working together to:

○ Understand strengths, challenges, and career aspirations
○ Define and clarify goals
○ Ensure necessary skills and experiences are acquired
○ Refine intangible skills for higher-level positions as desired
○ Support career aspirations

• • •

Now that you have a solid grasp of the coaching fundamentals, you're ready to explore how they combine to create highly effective coaching sessions that can ignite greatness in your team members.

# ESSENTIAL TAKEAWAYS

At the end of each chapter, you'll find Essential Takeaways. These are the most important points you'll need to carry into your professional life to find lasting success. In this chapter, the Essential Takeaways are:

- Workplace coaching is a personalized process that inspires employees to take control of their own development in a way that improves their performance now and maximizes their potential for success in the future.

- "Leader-coaches" aren't just leaders who deliver meaningful performance reviews. They coach their employees and have a highly specific approach to genuinely develop their team members in a targeted, ongoing way.

- Coaching will likely include some elements of managing, training, and mentoring rolled into it, but the primary goal of coaching is to make other people more successful.

- Coaches focus on the growth and well-being of their employees in a way that unlocks the potential of each individual. Instead of looking at what needs to be corrected, they look at what could be.

- *Performance Coaching* involves helping employees become more effective in their current jobs.

- *Developmental Coaching* is helping employees prepare to meet their long-term career goals.

**CHAPTER**

**2**

# Your Five-Step Model for Coaching

**All leaders bring their** unique approaches and personalities to the coaching process, but the most successful ones often follow some proven guidelines. This chapter delivers an underlying framework to help you define the regular interactions you have with anyone you coach—and it only requires five steps that you can start implementing today.

## STEP 1: ASSESS THE SITUATION

When it comes to Performance Coaching, the purpose of this step is to get the full picture of what's really happening with your coachee's current performance and to understand his or her development opportunities for the future. As you collect data in the coaching process, you can gather information from other colleagues and coworkers, performance metrics, or customer ratings.

You can also gather feedback by asking coachees directly and hearing their perspectives. Ask meaningful questions and look for circumstantial factors that may be affecting their performance. For example, are they facing a personal crisis at home? Do they have the right level of training and experience to be successful? Do they fully understand the way their progress is being measured? Do they have all the tools they need? Do they know how to use the new technology recently mandated by the company? What drives them?

By asking questions that help you understand your coachees better, you can dig beneath the surface, which is important because data alone will rarely guide you in your coaching journey together. This discovery process should be done in a neutral way, without making any assumptions. It's important for people who are being coached to feel comfortable expressing themselves, and your clear objectivity will invite them into a more open dialogue.

When it comes to Developmental Coaching, the "data" you gather might simply be observations you make and observations others make about your coachees. These insights will help you begin to identify your coachees' strengths and weaknesses. For instance, you may find that a strength that has gotten them noticed and rewarded in the past is being overemphasized to the point of making it a weakness.

• • •

Consider Amit, a compliance manager for a national building supply company. Amit was wicked smart and perfectly suited for his position. He was a voracious reader and somehow kept up with all of the industry's rapidly shifting regulations and legislative changes. The company was experiencing steady growth, and Amit ran a tight ship to minimize any liability that might undermine profitability.

This all sounds good except . . . Amit was also the one in the meetings who sucked the air right out of the room. He was so focused on pointing out the risks and roadblocks of a new solution or concept that he stifled any open exchange of ideas or alternatives.

Shanna, Amit's manager and coach, began to notice that people were less engaged and less willing to share in meetings that Amit attended. To avoid getting shut down by him, they simply shut themselves down. Brainstorming was limited, and innovation was curtailed.

As part of Shanna's initial coaching assessment, she looped Amit into the conversation by asking him to think about some key aspects of his role, using questions like these:

- "What do you think is your most important contribution to the team?"

- "What values and beliefs do you hold that impact the way you do your job?"

- "How do you want your colleagues to view your participation on the team?"

- "Do you think that translates accurately? Is that how they perceive you?"

- "Could there be any blind spots at play?"

With those answers, Shanna and Amit were able to fully assess his situation and collaboratively determine the challenges and opportunities ahead. Amit learned through his coaching sessions how to better manage his risk aversion and use it at appropriate times rather than continuously.

• • •

Whether you are collecting data or making observations, this first step allows you to create a solid foundation for the coaching experience together with your coachee. This is also a great time for you to agree on your coaching purpose: the behaviors in question, the performance metrics introduced, or the career goals discussed.

The goal of the assessment phase is to compare the current situation with the goal. Where are we now and where do we need to go? Once you've identified that gap together, you can begin searching for ways to close it.

## STEP 2: GENERATE IDEAS

After you and your employees have agreed on the challenges or opportunities at hand, together begin brainstorming strategies to make targeted improvements, resolve any problems, or close gaps.

The best thing you can do as a coach during this step is to help your coachees stretch their thinking and consider alternatives and approaches outside their usual frame of reference. Maybe that means sharing your own experiences to help spur new ideas or providing examples of others who faced similar challenges. Whatever route you take, push them to move beyond "business as usual."

Whenever possible, let your coachees come up with suggestions before you make any recommendations. Again, remain neutral—even if everything inside you wants to blurt out, "That will never work in a million years!" Let them explain their rationale and then encourage them to think through the implementation process. They will either come around to your same conclusion or, on occasion, convince you to think about the issue from a different perspective. Even if you start the conversation with a plan in mind, try to weave in your coachees' ideas to increase their ownership in the process.

If your coachees need a little help in coming up with solutions to improve, enhance, or move to the next level, try asking probing questions such as:

- "What are all the different ways you could reach your goal or close the gap?"

- "What are the pros and cons of each option?"

- "What factors will impact your ability to succeed?"

- "What risks are involved?" ("Are they worth it?")

- "Of all the options, which solution/approach gives you the best chance of success with the least risk?"

- "What resources would you need?"

- "What behaviors can you experiment with to adjust the way others experience you while working to reach your goal?"

The goal of Step 2 is to start a productive conversation that could trigger new ideas from those you coach and nudge them to explore a wider set of alternatives. By helping to push those boundaries, you can contribute to a pattern of more innovative thinking and stronger solutions.

## STEP 3: DEVELOP AN ACTION PLAN

Once you and your coachees have exhausted the possibilities and analyzed the options, it's time to work together to develop an action plan and set some concrete goals. When the people being coached take responsibility for identifying the actual game plan, they inevitably feel a greater sense of commitment to delivering a "win."

The action plan you set should specify deliverables and deadlines, as well as the strategies that need to be implemented. Be sure to agree on all of these terms, including the tools to get there and milestones that will be used to measure progress.

Let's look at a few examples to help illustrate this step.

• • •

Marcos was coaching Anna, a salesperson on his team. She was working hard, but her sales numbers were below the monthly targets. After a productive coaching conversation, Marcos worked with Anna to develop a performance-based coaching plan.

She committed to spend at least four hours every week exploring how she could serve her existing clients on a deeper level rather than focusing all of her time on new prospects. In 60 days, Marcos and Anna will evaluate the impact of that strategy on overall sales, repeat sales, and client satisfaction.

• • •

Next, let's circle back to the situation with Amit to see how Developmental Coaching plays out in Step 3. Through Shanna's coaching, Amit was beginning to see how his overzealous risk avoidance was not well received by his colleagues.

In his action plan, Amit committed to holding back his immediate concerns until he had time to think through the whole situation. They decided that when he's tempted to raise the red flag in a meeting, he will instead write down his thoughts and let them "marinate" before deciding whether to bring them to someone's attention. In six months,

Amit committed to launch a 360-degree assessment to determine how his colleagues and coworkers perceive his contributions.

## STEP 4: PROVIDE SUPPORT

Supporting your coachees can take a number of different forms, including:

- Offering continuous encouragement
- Providing resources to support their growth
- Opening doors and removing obstacles
- Communicating regularly

Let's dive deeper into each.

### Offering Continuous Encouragement

As part of the coaching process, you will likely be pushing your employees out of their comfort zones—which often involves some setbacks. This means they'll need emotional support from you to maintain their momentum. This may also mean you'll need to make yourself available for additional one-on-one time or be open to sharing some of your experiences (positive and negative) in real time. A little vulnerability from you can go a long way here. By revealing some of your own struggles, you may be able to show that persistence pays off and give them the confidence to keep pushing forward.

Part of your job as a leader-coach is also to help coachees reconnect with what drives them, remember their goals, and revisit the benefits of progressing through their plans. This can involve being part cheerleader (helping them celebrate small wins) and part tough-love advisor (acting as an accountability partner). Both of those roles require an ample amount of encouragement.

It takes time and energy to sustain this type of ongoing support, especially when your calendar is jammed and you've got your own deliverables. But it really is the key to getting the results you want from the coaching experience.

## Providing Resources to Support Their Growth

Pay close attention to determine what your employees need as it relates to their learning and development agendas. What targeted resources could help them reach their goals? It's not as simple as providing them with a list of books that might be helpful or telling them to sign up for a class. No two coachees will ever need exactly the same resources. Every person is different, and every goal is different.

As a coach, you'll want to customize the resources you provide or recommend based on the needs of each individual. You might provide access to selected professional development courses, webinars, books, rotation groups, an additional mentor, or even more of your time.

Another thing to keep in mind is that the coaching relationship is a partnership. Your employees may have a better idea of what resources would be most impactful for them. Remain open to their suggestions. If those ideas make sense, your role might simply be to obtain the necessary approvals.

## Opening Doors and Removing Obstacles

Sometimes your coachees will face challenges that require your support. Some obstacles might include budget limitations, uncooperative colleagues, sparse resources, or lack of internal connections.

If your coachee is lacking internal connections, one of the best questions you can ask your him or her is: "Who else could participate in helping you meet your goal?" Introducing your employees to people who have faced similar challenges or have access to a particular data platform that could prove useful to them might just be one of the most valuable contributions you can make as a coach.

When it makes sense, use your tenure and clout to make connections on behalf of the people you coach so they can leverage that knowledge and experience learning from a broader set of professionals. Opening doors and making the right introductions can frequently add significant value.

There will also be times when only you can help your coachee plow through roadblocks. It's important to remember these obstacles may present themselves in diverse fashions, but they all have the insidious potential to drag down the performance of those you coach:

- **Skill deficits:** lack of training, difficulty with new technology

- **Poor communication:** misunderstanding goals or situations because of mixed messages or inadequate documentation

- **Organizational barriers:** uncooperative colleagues, scheduling problems, time zone differences, remote work challenges

- **Personal circumstances:** experiencing illness, being a single parent, caring for an elderly parent, going through a divorce

Find out what's getting in the way and make a plan to remove it (or help coachees get around it). Perhaps that involves adjusting coachees' priorities, shifting their schedules, getting them the additional training they need, or arranging for them to take on stretch assignments.

## Communicating Regularly

The most effective coaches maintain open lines of communication with their employees along their journey together. That's what keeps the process alive. I'm not referring just to formal exchanges of information that happen because they're scheduled on the Outlook calendar. This ties back to the relationships at the heart of the coaching. Leader-coaches with excellent communication skills make a point to touch base with a quick text, follow up with a short phone call, or spontaneously offer to grab some coffee and talk about how things are going.

The lesson here? To succeed as a coach, stay involved and stay connected. Even if you're crazy busy. *Especially* if you're crazy busy! Coaching simply can't work if the employees you're working with feel abandoned.

When you communicate regularly, you demonstrate your commitment to providing support in a variety of ways and pave a path for your team members to achieve accelerated growth—while also reaping a multitude of benefits as the coach.

## STEP 5: FOLLOW UP

Aside from sporadic coaching on the go, set regular dates to formally check in with your coachees with a structured conversation. During these official check-ins, discuss their progress, analyze any potential setbacks, and refine areas for professional development. If you detect any issues, use those regular touchpoints to course correct as needed.

• • •

Following these five steps will provide the structure needed to keep your coaching conversations on track and your outcomes productive.

And, in an ideal world, all of these steps would occur in the same meeting. However, if you sense your coachee needs time to reflect and process (or feels overwhelmed), schedule a follow-up meeting to close the loop on any of these steps.

## YOUR FIVE-STEP MODEL IN ACTION

Now that we know the five steps for effective coaching, let's see what this process looks like in action. And, be sure to reference this illustration any time you need a reminder of the steps.

1. Assess the situation

2. Generate ideas

3. Develop an action plan

4. Provide support

5. Follow up

Now, imagine that you're coaching a team member named Leo. He has been with the company for four years and has proven to be a valued employee in your department for the past 14 months. He is smart, proactive, and a steady contributor to the team.

Last week, you checked in with Keenan, another team member, for an update on one of the group projects. Much to your surprise, Keenan launched into quite a rant about Leo! He essentially blamed the lack of progress and likelihood of missing their deadline on Leo's attitude and inability to think about alternate solutions with an open mind. While missing that deadline would be a huge problem, the bigger issue is Leo and Keenan will need to collaborate again long after this project is finished.

## Step 1: Assess the Situation

As part of your assessment, you check in on the status of Leo's other projects and discover that those are on target. No one else has any complaints about him. You also look at Leo's recent work to see if there are any huge fluctuations when it comes to deliverables that may have impacted Leo's patience or attitude. Nothing out of the norm there either. To continue your assessment, you schedule a meeting with Leo and prepare the following questions for him, starting general and getting more specific:

"How are things going for you these days?"

"Is the project moving forward as you expected?"

"Is there anything in particular slowing you down?"

Leo responds to the initial question saying that everything is fine, and he is looking forward to spending time with his family during the upcoming holidays.

As you work through the next few questions, you begin to get Leo's side of the story.

Leo tells you that progress is slower than he anticipated because he and Keenan can't seem to agree on the best plan of action. He explains matter-of-factly that Keenan doesn't seem to understand the best way forward is to follow the protocol that Leo put in place for similar product launches. He is frustrated by having to spend so much time trying to get Keenan on board, and he decided to avoid another meeting in hopes that Keenan would come to his senses. Leo seems relatively unfazed by the situation.

In response, you ask Leo to describe Keenan's preferred strategy. Leo throws out a few comments without much detail, making it apparent that he hasn't fully listened to Keenan's ideas. Even though Leo has remained calm and collected about the situation, his less-than-collaborative approach is dragging down progress on a critical project.

Using everything you have learned from Leo and those around him, you can discuss the situation with greater clarity and establish some goals. Those include staying on track with the product launch, leveraging the experiences and thought processes of both team members, and developing a more collaborative relationship.

To jump-start the next phase, you offer Leo some advice. You remind him that, despite disagreeing on specific strategies, he and Keenan still share common goals. If they can use those as a starting point for their next conversation, they may find a more productive path forward.

## Step 2: Generate Ideas

Next, you ask Leo some questions to help him reflect on the situation and gauge his willingness to collaborate more openly:

"How can you create the conditions for a more constructive meeting with Keenan?"

"What could you do to demonstrate to Keenan that you are genuinely interested in his perspective?"

"How can you show Keenan that you respect him and his ideas, even if you have differences of opinion?"

"How would you be willing to compromise with Keenan on the strategy and still feel good about it yourself?"

Through the discussion prompted by these questions, Leo generates a number of different solutions to help get the project back on track. Together you sort through which ones are viable and which are less likely to achieve the desired results.

## Step 3: Develop an Action Plan

Based on the ideas Leo discussed with you, he commits to setting up a meeting with Keenan by the end of the week. His plan is to recalibrate the situation by focusing on their common goals as a starting point, and he will listen attentively to Keenan's perspective. More importantly, Leo makes the commitment to integrate some of Keenan's ideas into the launch strategy.

Leo also sees the value in building a better working relationship with Keenan, and he wants to begin laying the groundwork for that. Instead of suggesting they meet on a Zoom dial-in only call, he opts for a Zoom video meeting so he can better read Keenan's body language and make a better attempt at conveying interest. In between these discussions, he will make an effort to get to know Keenan a little better as a person.

Finally, Leo agrees to report back to you on the meeting results with a firm rollout strategy for the product launch, complete with milestones and ownership tags.

## Step 4: Provide Support

You feel fairly confident that this conversation will smooth things over between Leo and Keenan, but you offer to step in if the meeting doesn't go as anticipated. You make yourself available before they meet in case Leo wants to run anything by you in advance. You suggest that Leo could find out more about the best ways to work with Keenan by reaching out to Yamini who has been Keenan's partner on numerous projects over the years and might have some helpful insights.

## Step 5: Follow Up

You mark your calendar to touch base with Leo the following Wednesday if you haven't heard from him before then with an update on the situation.

● ● ●

So what was the outcome? Leo got some great advice from Yamini and, as a result, Leo and Keenan had a productive meeting. Even though they still didn't see eye to eye on everything, they kept their shared goals top of mind and adopted a more collaborative approach. As a coach, you can feel relieved that these two savvy professionals were able to come together for the sake of meeting the objectives. Even better, you didn't have to step in to moderate any negative interactions.

## PUTTING THE STEPS TOGETHER

This five-step coaching framework provides an easy, intuitive road map to guide your conversations with employees. But make no mistake, it's not a one-size-fits-all solution. Coaching isn't always a linear process, and some aspects of the framework won't be necessary or appropriate for certain situations. For example, you may not need to cover all the steps if you are coaching informally between meetings.

On the other hand, this framework still gives you a strong edge as a coach. Knowing you have these steps as a guide can help you assume a coaching mindset, which is incredibly important when you are juggling managerial duties and your own deliverables.

The framework can also be used as a tool to help you measure your own effectiveness as a coach. Are you touching on each step when it makes sense? Are you overemphasizing some? Maybe you're skipping others? Even if you approach the framework with flexibility, you can use it as a checklist to make sure you are giving your coachees the full spectrum of guidance they need to be successful.

You'll find a summary of these five steps in the Coaching Essentials Toolkit at the back of the book.

## ESSENTIAL TAKEAWAYS

- Step 1 of your coaching model is *Assess the Situation*. The purpose of this step is to get the full picture of what's really happening with your coachees' current performance and understand their development opportunities for the future.

- Step 2 of your coaching model is *Generate Ideas*. The best thing you can do as a coach during this step is to help your coachees stretch their thinking and consider alternatives and approaches outside their usual frame of reference.

- Step 3 of your coaching model is *Develop an Action Plan*. When your coachees take responsibility for identifying the actual game plan, they inevitably feel a greater sense of commitment to delivering a "win."

- Step 4 of your coaching model is *Provide Support*. This can mean offering continuous encouragement, providing resources to support their growth, opening doors, removing any obstacles, and communicating regularly.

- Step 5 of your coaching model is *Follow Up*. Aside from sporadic coaching on the go, set regular dates to formally check in with your coachees with a structured conversation.

# Coaching Skills

**With your five-step coaching** model from Chapter 2 as a backdrop, it's time to layer in the actual coaching skills necessary to be successful in this role. These skills include:

- Building trust and rapport

- Using questions strategically

- Listening intently

- Suspending judgment

- Delivering feedback

- Challenging appropriately

- Setting actionable goals

Let's take a closer look at each of these skills separately.

## BUILDING TRUST AND RAPPORT

Several years ago, I got together for dinner with a friend of mine who leads a project team. She tossed out a comment in passing: "I just wish I could help my team be more engaged and more productive." Well, this wasn't an official consulting session (and there might have been a glass of wine involved), but I decided to toss out an idea I thought would be helpful.

I suggested she consider having more one-on-one check-ins with her team members versus trying to fully connect with them during group meetings alone. She could ask how they're doing and provide them with more individual input. About that time, the waiter delivered our bruschetta, and we moved on to discuss something else.

A few months later, I touched base with my friend to ask how things were going. She laughed and said my suggestion was a total and complete . . . flop.

What?!? Not at all what I expected to hear.

She explained that she started scheduling one-on-ones with her staff members the day after our dinner. In every meeting, she asked direct questions like "What challenges are you facing right now?," "What type of support do you need?," "Could I offer you some feedback on your performance?"

She proceeded to say there were no words to describe how incredibly awkward those interactions were. I believe she used a couple of phrases like "deer in headlights," "completely baffled," and "downright suspicious." It was obvious these employees had no idea where this conversation was coming from nor why she suddenly wanted that information.

I knew right then and there that I had made a mistake. I had jumped into "fix-it mode" without asking more questions. The first one should have been: "How well do you really know these employees?" And her answer would have been, "Not very well." No wonder they looked at her like she was crazy!

The most important coaching skill—and the one that has to come before all others—is to build trust and rapport with your team members. These form the foundation of everything else you will do as a coach.

The problem is, leaders are wired to be efficient. We want to fix whatever's wrong and find the fastest way to solve the problem. I did that myself, without even thinking, when I gave my friend some advice.

It takes time to get to know people on a deeper level and build real relationships with them. But without that connection as a starting point, coaching is doomed to fail. Here are two pivotal ways to begin the process of building rapport and trust.

## Make Yourself More Approachable

In strong coaching relationships, coachees feel comfortable talking about their vulnerabilities, challenges, fears, and concerns. That level of honesty can't happen if employees feel intimidated or inferior.

Great coaches have a way of making themselves more approachable while also putting other people at ease. They come to the table as someone who has others' best interests at heart, not just trying to find the easiest, fastest solution.

For obvious reasons, you want to have coaching conversations in person, whether that means face-to-face in the office or via cameras on Zoom. So much of how we interpret someone's message is based on what we can see. If you remove that option, you leave more room for misinterpretation and limit your ability to send signals of warmth, authenticity, and caring.

Once you're in full view (be it in person or on camera), pay close attention to your facial expressions, body language, demeanor, and tone of voice. Avoid crossing your arms or giving the impression that you're "closed off." If you sound terse or irritable, your approachability score takes a huge dive.

When it's possible, make yourself available for some spur-of-the-moment meetings, too. If you're on-site, you might even schedule time to walk through the office and check on your employees. If you are working virtually, consider holding "open office hours"—a regularly scheduled time and day of the week when any of your team members can log in to Zoom or Teams and get your full attention. Availability often bleeds into approachability, which creates a deeper coaching bond.

## Show Genuine Interest in the People You Coach

Take the time to learn more about the people you coach. Sounds simple, right?

The obvious part here is getting to know their career profiles, which includes their professional strengths and weaknesses, hidden talents, development needs, and job aspirations. Those components will naturally emerge as part of your coaching conversations.

The bigger challenge for building rapport and trust is getting to know them as humans, not just employees. While that comes easily for some people, others need more of a game plan. Here's an example of what that looks like in action.

Ross had just started coaching several new people on his team, and he made a point of asking about their interests and hobbies. He discovered some fascinating facts. Brenda sometimes sells her oil paintings on Etsy. Marvin regularly participates in open-mic night at the local comedy club. Shelley is training for the New York City Marathon.

Ross also wanted to know a little more about the families of his new coachees. He found out that Shelley's son is on a soccer team that's playing in the state tournament. Brenda's twin brother is finally in remission after fighting lung cancer for two years. Marvin's daughter is about to graduate from high school and headed to The University of Texas in Austin.

While Ross had the best of intentions, he knew that the chances of remembering those details the following week were slim to none. So, after each coaching session, he spent a few minutes privately jotting down the pertinent facts for reference.

Forgive the melodrama here, but those small efforts helped to make Ross a trust-and-rapport-building ninja.

With a quick glance at his notes, he could start the next coaching session with a personalized question that demonstrated his interest in their lives:

- "How's the training process going for the marathon?"

- "What kinds of things have you been painting these days?"

- "How is your brother doing?"

- "When are you moving your daughter to Austin?"

*Zing!* He cared enough to *ask* and *listen*. He *remembered* (even with a little assistance). And he *followed up!* And, he did it in a way that was anything but disingenuous. He formed a new habit for connecting on a personal level that will eventually become second nature.

The people you're coaching will know that you care if you use this process to become more familiar with the things that really matter to them and demonstrate your genuine interest over time.

One other thing—as you break the ice, be prepared to answer your coachees' questions in response. If you expect them to share, you'll need to do the same. That back-and-forth works wonders to create an environment where your coachees feel a growing sense of trust.

## USING QUESTIONS STRATEGICALLY

I had been coaching Nathan, a director from a major insurance company, for about three months. I could tell that he understood the basic components of coaching his team, but he was having trouble getting traction and wasn't seeing any significant results. I asked if I could observe some of his interactions with direct reports, and he agreed.

One of Nathan's meetings was with Elizabeth, a bright young project manager who had more enthusiasm than experience. Her fearless attitude prompted her to eagerly volunteer for special assignments and take on the tasks nobody else wanted. As admirable as that might sound, Elizabeth also occasionally found herself in over her head.

She was currently working on a project that could determine whether the entire team would complete a critical deliverable. Nathan hadn't received a status update, and he was getting concerned. I was in his office when Elizabeth walked in for their meeting.

**Nathan:** "How's the project going?"

**Elizabeth:** "Pretty well!"

**Nathan:** "Great. Any problems I should know about?"

**Elizabeth:** "No, not right now."

**Nathan:** "Are you planning to talk to the people in John's department, or did you decide that wasn't necessary?"

**Elizabeth:** "I certainly can. I'll add that to my list!"

**Nathan:** "Sounds good. Please keep me posted."

I was stunned. By the speed of the meeting. By the lack of depth in the dialogue. By the absence of urgency surrounding such an important part of the team's project.

I knew I had to give Nathan a crash course on how to use questions strategically.

I walked Nathan through the parallels between coaching and the precise actions of seasoned archeologists. These historians often work from a map, and they know where to dig to find the best artifacts. They proceed very carefully so as not to disturb anything in the excavation process. There is no random use of the shovel just because they reached a convenient spot—ever. They are always methodical and thorough.

Great leader-coaches use a similar approach by getting strategic with their use of questions. The process is targeted, structured, engaging, and efficient. They understand that the quality of their coaching sessions will be determined by the quality of their questions. If they ask vague, random questions (like Nathan had done), they are unlikely to uncover anything of value.

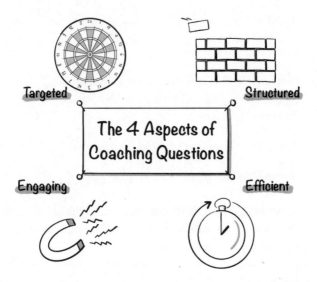

I could tell that Nathan needed more of a map, so I walked him through the different types of questions he could ask.

## Open-Ended Questions

First and foremost, Nathan needed to switch up the actual format he uses for many of his questions.

Whether you are coaching someone or trying to make small talk at a cocktail party, nothing brings the conversation to a screeching halt like questions that can be answered with a single word—also known as closed-ended questions. To be fair, sometimes they do serve a purpose, especially when you just want a short, definitive response. ("Did the client call yet?" "No.")

But for coaching purposes, using open-ended questions will encourage more discussion and potentially lead to additional questions and answers.

| *Closed-Ended Questions* | *Open-Ended Questions* |
|---|---|
| "How are you today?" ("Fine!") | "What did you do this weekend?" |
| "How's the project going?" ("Great!") | "How would you describe your progress on the project right now?" |
| "Will you meet the deadline?" ("Yes!") | "What obstacles might prevent you from meeting the deadline?" |

This seems like a simple adjustment, but many people say it takes ongoing effort to make open-ended questions part of their regular conversation toolkits.

## Targeted Prompts

While Nathan agreed about the value of the open-ended format, he was a little concerned that the nonstop questions might make him sound like an investigative journalist. I assured him he had options.

As an alternative, sometimes coaches can use targeted prompts to get the same results as from open-ended questions. While not technically questions, phrases like these can also open the door for more extended conversations about a particular topic:

"Tell me more about . . . "

"Describe the current situation with . . . "

"Give me the latest update on . . . "

## Questions by Categories

Nathan could also add variety to his coaching conversations by blending in different types of questions while he digs for information and insight. Three helpful question categories are fact-finding, thought-provoking, and comprehension.

### Fact-Finding Questions

These questions allow coaches to gather the facts they need to assess a situation. The answers help coaches understand the current landscape, assumptions, problems, and opportunities.

> "What was your sales total from last month?"

> "Did the vendor deliver on time?"

> "What challenges are you facing right now?"

> "How is our biggest competitor responding to this problem?"

### Thought-Provoking Questions

These questions prompt coachees to think outside the box and consider fresh approaches. When coaches use them, they help their employees stretch beyond their comfort zones, shake up their usual approaches, rethink their assumptions, consider overlooked factors, and reflect on new ways to achieve their goals:

> "How would you solve this problem if you didn't have to consider . . . ?"

> "What if you took a completely different approach to . . . ?"

> "What are we missing here?"

> "How is this helping to move you closer to your goal?"

*Comprehension Questions*

These questions allow coaches to gauge their employees' awareness and understanding of the situation. Questions like the following provide a barometer for the information that is already known and areas that need further exploration:

"What are the pros and cons of that decision?"

"What do you think is the likely outcome if you proceed with that approach?"

"What is your back-up plan?"

"What skills and attributes will you need for the role you hope to get next? And how can you prepare for that?"

By strategically asking these different types of questions (open-ended, targeted, fact-finding, thought-provoking, and comprehension), you uncover a higher quality of information that allows you to coach more effectively.

## LISTENING INTENTLY

While asking questions allows you to uncover helpful insights and generate genuine connections with your mentees, they won't be effective unless you listen intently.

Imagine a football team in the locker room at halftime. The players are battling their biggest rival and are currently behind by two touchdowns. They gather around the coach, who shares a motivational message—one that will hopefully inspire them to go out and win the game. The coach speaks with great emotion and uses dramatic pauses for effect.

You've probably watched this scene in dozens of TV shows and movies. While it often makes for some great storytelling, it also perpetuates the idea that coaching is all about speaking passionately and saying the right things. But, what is the role of the people being coached? To sit still and listen.

The truth is this Hollywood stereotype doesn't translate to coaching in the business world. Why? Because one of the most important coaching skills is listening—active, intense listening.

Don't get me wrong. Your *communication style* is certainly important as a coach, but you can significantly improve your impact by adding finesse to your *listening style*.

If you want to become a stronger coach, here are five strategies you can use to enhance your listening skills: adjust your frame of mind, deliberately stay focused, demonstrate actively listening, pay attention to find any disconnects, and summarize and paraphrase.

## Adjust Your Frame of Mind

This strategy takes some practice and discipline. Before starting your coaching sessions, try to get into the right mindset. Remind yourself that *their* success is a *shared* success. Their performance improvements also reflect positively on you. Your position as a coach is to be *on their side*, to be their advocate, and to be their accountability system. That will set the stage for effective listening.

Then, as your coaching sessions begin, take a deep breath, and adjust your pace. Be patient and let employees finish rather than cutting them off in mid-sentence, even if you know what they're going to say. Don't jump in with advice or volunteer the answer. Listen from the perspective of a partner who is fully invested in their success. Having the right mindset allows you to listen with greater purpose.

## Deliberately Stay Focused

Distractions are everywhere. All around us and even inside our heads. These distractions have an annoying way of hijacking our ability to listen with the full power of our brains. Start by asking yourself honestly if any of these descriptions apply to you when you're having a significant, face-to-face conversation with someone:

- You stop paying attention because you're thinking about the point you want to make next.

- You get sidetracked by everything going on around you: email notifications, phones ringing, unopened mail, people walking by your office, the dinner reservation you forgot to make.

- You find yourself becoming judgmental and discounting their ideas after you notice some errors in their messages.

- You start to feel irritated when they can't stay on topic or get to the point.

- You stop hearing the words because you are concentrating so hard on an exit strategy.

Those statements resonate with many people because, yes, listening can be tough. But, when it comes to coaching, leaders have to work hard to overcome those tendencies. Focus. Get your head in the game and, at least temporarily, try to block out everything else.

Be proactive about removing any potential distractions during a coaching session. Put away your phone. Silence your computer. Hold the meeting in a location that minimizes interruptions. And then commit to listening with a laser focus.

## Demonstrate Actively Listening

While you work on being mentally engaged, be sure your body language isn't sending a different message. If you're slouching in your chair and staring out the window while your coachees are talking—even if you *are* listening—they may wonder if you are thinking about your weekend plans rather than their current challenges.

Lean forward slightly and take notes on their comments. Make eye contact, and nod occasionally to indicate you are following their train of thought. Don't fidget. And, most importantly, try to avoid interrupting.

I know the last point is a huge temptation—especially when someone has gone off on an irrelevant tangent. We can think 10 times faster than we can speak, so our brains sometimes get a little bored when we are playing the role of listener. Our wandering minds tend to jump ahead, prompting us to think of other ideas, objections, or key points. Then before we know it, we have blurted those out and derailed the conversation. It's not easy, but do everything you can to stay in focused listening mode and demonstrate that you are "plugged in."

## Pay Attention to Find Any Disconnects

As you listen, identify any areas that sound vague, confusing, or contradictory. Is there anything that just doesn't add up? After they have finished their statements, ask employees for clarification. By prompting them to further explain a situation or decision, you can uncover critical information about the project or process. Identifying those disconnects through listening can also provide you with golden opportunities for some teachable moments.

## Summarize and Paraphrase

This is one of the best strategies coaches can use to fully focus and listen during time with team members. At the end of a session, great coaches provide a concise summary of the conversation by paraphrasing the employees' comments and confirming what they heard.

I've found that many leaders feel this step is unnecessary or even gratuitous, but you might be surprised at the value it adds. People derive benefits from hearing someone else recap what they've said. Sometimes it helps them to put structure around their own thinking, to tighten their messaging, or to view things from a different perspective. Without strong listening skills, you can't add that value and position yourself as a genuine thinking partner.

• • •

Strategic listening may take time to perfect, but it is a must-have tool for coaches who want to make a positive impact. I can't emphasize that enough. Invest the time and energy to improve your listening style, and you will be rewarded with increased coaching success.

## SUSPENDING JUDGMENT

If you've watched any courtroom dramas, you know there are usually scowling judges who reprimand overly eager attorneys for "leading the witness"—guiding the testimony to elicit certain comments that could sway the outcome in their favor. While your coaching sessions won't involve a scowling judge, the lesson is the same.

It can be difficult to suspend judgment, but try to enter every coaching conversation from a neutral position. No agendas. No biases.

No assumptions. Set all of that aside and focus on how you can help these employees improve and succeed. You do this by maintaining a positive attitude, releasing negative impressions, and pushing yourself to assume positive intent.

## Maintain a Positive Attitude

Before we ever get to any judgment about the person being coached, we have to start with *you*. Awkward, huh? If you enter every coaching session with these thoughts running through your mind, you are destined to fail:

> *I'm not cut out for this.*
>
> *Nothing I can say will make a difference.*
>
> *This person doesn't care, so it's a waste of time.*

You'll never generate any momentum if that's the fuel you're using. Instead, assume your coaching conversations will be the exact spark needed to move an employee forward to do amazing things, to change a thought process, to adjust behavior, or to find the courage to try a new approach. You're doing the work now to be prepared for this task, so go in with a positive attitude. You can do this!

## Release Any Negative Impressions

Perhaps the person you have been asked to coach has a less-than-stellar reputation. You've heard some reports about questionable behavior through the office grapevine. Nothing is confirmed, but there is a set of assumptions that may affect your view of the coachee. Or maybe you've got firsthand experience with this person and have serious doubts about any willingness to change or desire to progress.

The only way to mentally step into the role of a coach—a partner and advocate—is to block out those preconceived ideas or negative impressions. If those assumptions (which could be false) are crowding your thoughts, your heart probably won't be in it. Even worse, you'll certainly have a tough time convincing the coachee of your dedication.

## Push Yourself to Assume Positive Intent

You can file this one in the folder labeled "benefit of the doubt." Inevitably the people you coach will say or do something that is wrong or shows an error in judgment. Remind yourself that they did not purposely make a mistake. (If they did, that's a completely different issue.) Assume that their decisions or actions were logical to them and based on the information they had at the time. They may have failed, but you'll be a better coach if you assume they were trying to do the right thing.

If assuming positive intent is too ambitious, at least shoot for a neutral response. Consider it to be a challenge, and search for a different perspective that will contradict your initial impressions. Looking at the situation from their angle, how did they make that choice? Get to know them and find out where they are coming from.

The only way you can find the best in those you coach is to view them through a positive lens. Suspend your judgment and block out the negativity.

## DELIVERING FEEDBACK

Feedback is one of my favorite topics. I firmly believe it's a powerful tool that can help us expand our self-awareness and make sure our intent matches our impact on others.

I often speak to audiences about the importance of getting feedback, and years ago I developed a proprietary online tool to help my clients do just that. This 360-degree survey platform is simple and effective, and it allows professionals to get anonymous feedback from the people they work with most often—supervisors, colleagues, and direct reports.

Here's the interesting thing. At the end of my presentations, all the attendees in the room seem to agree about the value of feedback for career advancement. Since I frequently offer my survey tool to them free of charge, I ask who might be interested. Every hand in the room goes up. But the actual number of people who take advantage of this free resource? A measly 10 percent. That's the average over a decade.

Apparently *knowing you could benefit from feedback* and *actually asking for it* are two very different things.

What's happening there? According to behavioral scientists, we want to learn and grow—but we also want to be accepted just the way we are. Besides, we are often afraid of what people are going to tell us if they are honest. Will we be embarrassed? Shocked? Offended? How do we know if there is a hidden agenda behind their comments?

Getting feedback can make us anxious. We tend to take it personally, not purposefully. And if we've had negative experiences with it in the past, we try to avoid it at all costs.

Keep that context in mind as you deliver feedback to your coachees. They may be extremely uncomfortable.

You can set the tone for productive feedback sessions with your coachees by demonstrating that all feedback isn't negative. In fact, you build their confidence by pointing out some of the things they are doing really, really well. Maybe they have some behaviors or attributes that others admire. Highlighting those and providing positive reinforcement will help them play to their individual strengths.

When addressing areas for improvement, approach those subjects with an abundance of emotional intelligence. Be patient, kind, and respectful. Choose your words and tone of voice carefully. Then pay close attention to their responses to your messages. Watch closely for their reactions to your statements and make adjustments in real time if you sense they are anxious or uncomfortable. *How* you say something is just as important as *what* you say.

To help you improve your feedback skills and your impact as a coach, here are five guidelines to follow.

### Feedback should always be...

Specific

Timely

Purposeful

Tactful

Ongoing

## Feedback Should Be Specific

Instead of saying something general like, "I've noticed that you tend to be critical of your coworkers," provide examples. "During the 3:30

meeting yesterday, you dismissed Shawn's idea, and it seemed like you were uninterested in his perspective. Was that your intent?"

Don't assume you know what they're thinking. Ask. Focus on observable actions and stick to facts rather than your assumptions. Make sure you link your feedback to a specific outcome, too: What's the result of the behavior you are discussing?

An example of this in action? "I heard great things about you from the client this morning. That new, weekly follow-up strategy is working!" The employee changed a behavior, and the result is greater client satisfaction.

Here's another: "I just met with Gary in accounting, and I'm concerned they don't have all the information they need from you to process the quarterly updates." The employee failed to turn in a report, and that is having a negative effect on another department. Be specific and highlight why your employee's behavior matters.

## Feedback Should Be Timely

If it's October and your employees have a huge win (or a behavioral problem), that feedback shouldn't wait until the March performance review. They need to know that you, as the coach, notice what's going on in real time. It's your job either to celebrate with them or to guide them in making immediate improvements. Don't wait.

With that said, coaching in real time doesn't involve blurting out a reprimand in the lunchroom. Select the right time and place to share that information. Make sure the environment will put the employee at ease, and provide enough space in the schedule for adequate discussion. Just do it sooner rather than later.

## Feedback Should Be Purposeful

When providing feedback, focus on helping employees improve, grow, or develop. Before you deliver suggestions or constructive criticism, think about some key questions:

- *What is the purpose of this information?*

- *Is it relevant?*

- *It is usable?*

- *Could it make a difference in their performance or ability to reach their goals?*

By answering those questions *before* you start providing feedback, you can frame the conversation so it feels helpful and targeted rather than critical or petty.

For example, "I'm sharing this with you because I know you want to improve your sales numbers, and I believe this is an important adjustment that can help you do that."

To employees, that approach shows that you care about them and their goals. It proves you want to help them, which compels them to listen to your message in a very different way.

## Feedback Should Be Tactful

Delivering negative feedback can be awkward, but employees can't improve if they don't know what needs to change. Remember to keep the emphasis on the problematic behavior or situation instead of implying that someone is a bad person.

When you're ready to provide feedback, ask for permission to share your concerns:

"Are you open to hearing what I observed?"

"Can I provide my perspective?"

Keep your emotions in check and be careful with your word choices. It also helps if you try to start your sentences with "I" rather than "you" to minimize defensiveness.

For example, "I am concerned about the tone you used with the client on the phone this morning." That has a completely different impact than saying, "You are way too abrupt."

## Feedback Should Be Ongoing

In a beneficial coaching relationship, feedback needs to be a regular part of your ongoing conversations. It's not a one-time event. As trust develops, offer real-time feedback in formal and informal settings rather than only at scheduled meetings. The point is, don't assume your employees can accurately judge their own performance.

The best way for employees to grow is by having a coach who is tuned in and paying close attention to their work. They will respect someone who cares enough about their success to speak up when their performance deserves a high five or an honest assessment of what went wrong. Your coaching feedback may be exactly what they need to build on their strengths and minimize their weaknesses.

One final note about ongoing feedback. Even though coaches try to guide their employees to solve their own problems rather than providing the answers, there may be situations that warrant shifting immediately into corrective action mode. Perhaps a team member blatantly violates a company policy or somehow endangers a co-worker. That's the time to move quickly from the role of coach to that of manager. Take action and follow your company's escalation policy to correct the problem.

• • •

When coaches consistently deliver purposeful feedback that is specific, timely, and compassionate, employees quickly develop the skills they need to accelerate their careers.

## CHALLENGING APPROPRIATELY

Claire was a regional director for a packaged goods company, and she began coaching Hector, a junior manager. Three months into their coaching relationship, Claire was impressed with Hector's professionalism. He had a strong analytical background, his work was consistently thorough, and he had mentioned his desire to play a bigger role in the department's evolution.

Despite all of that, Claire began to recognize that Hector approached every single problem with the same solution. Step 1: Gather data. Step 2: Create a report. It was all very cut-and-dried. He had settled into a mental rut, despite his natural intelligence and incredible attention to detail. If Hector truly wanted to be an emerging leader, he could benefit from disrupting his typical approach and his usual pattern of thinking.

Claire's objective as a coach became clear—to appropriately challenge Hector's assumptions and perceptions, while nudging him to explore new possibilities. Perhaps there were underlying disconnects that needed to be addressed for Hector to be more successful. For example, Claire needed to push him to see some alternatives:

- His viewpoint of how colleagues reacted to something he did *versus* the actual impact he had

- His commitment to invest time on a certain development area *versus* how he really spent his time

Challenging Hector to see a wide range of things through a fresh lens could provide the fuel he needed to accelerate his growth and to be better prepared for the next level.

There are two ways you can challenge people appropriately—ask questions that expand the thinking process and choose your boundary challenges wisely.

## Ask Questions That Expand the Thinking Process

In their coaching sessions, Claire focused the discussion on disrupting Hector's usual thought processes. Here are some of the questions she posed over several coaching sessions:

- "What was your perception of what happened? And are you open to hearing what I observed and how it impacted others?"

- "How would you normally approach this problem? And what are the alternatives?"

- "How could a different approach give your solution more depth and texture?"

- "Who could you get involved to articulate a different point of view or even some objections?"

- "What do you have to lose if you try something different?"

- "What is your biggest concern about switching up your usual approach?"

- "What are you doing now to sharpen your skills and support your goal to advance within the company? And could you be inadvertently doing something that is holding you back? May I share my perspective?"

Claire deliberately pushed him outside his comfort zone. As you might guess, Hector resisted change at first. But Claire continued prompting him to tackle problems from a different angle. She was pleasantly surprised to discover that he took her advice on his latest project. Instead of just showing up with mountains of data for an in-house strategy meeting, he invited Meena from sales to participate in the conversation. Meena was able to add rich context about the customer experience that would have been lost if Hector relied solely on his spreadsheets.

Claire counted that as a huge win. The irony here? Claire thought her goal was to help Hector *do something*. As it turned out, she just needed to help him *do something different*.

## Choose Your Boundary Challenges Wisely

As you begin coaching your team members, be bold about challenging them when it's relatively safe for them to explore new territory. Some situations admittedly do warrant more caution. But when the time is right, provide the encouragement they need to move beyond the typical boundaries.

Your challenges might involve pointing out that they are trapped in a certain belief system that isn't serving them well, making false assumptions that are holding them back, or operating with "blinders" that prevent them from seeing other perspectives. Your job is to help them grow by prompting them to challenge their own thinking, to shake up the way they do things, and to question some of their unproductive beliefs. They will have a much better chance to succeed in pushing boundaries if they learn to challenge themselves, their typical approaches, and their own perceptions.

## SETTING ACTIONABLE GOALS

Jordan worked for a major automotive parts distribution company and loved his job as a senior manager. His personality—a blend of hearty enthusiasm and genuine sensitivity—made him a popular leader and an inspiring coach for the 13 people on his team. The problem? Jordan wasn't getting the same boost in performance from coaching as some of his less-personable counterparts.

Olivia, director of his division, began asking some questions to see if she could find the disconnect.

Here's what she discovered. Jordan was passionate about motivating his employees, seeing them get more engaged with their projects, and helping them grow and advance their careers. But he fell short when it came to attaching some quantifiable goals. He felt like it was a mistake to interrupt all the support and forward momentum with performance metrics and measurements. That just felt like a wet blanket.

Olivia appreciated his honesty but also knew Jordan was missing the main point.

Goal setting (or, more specifically, goal *achieving*) is the primary reason behind coaching. That's what makes the investment of time and effort pay off. Olivia reminded Jordan that the coaching relationship always needs to be rooted in purpose: to elevate the employees' skills, improve their performance, and prepare them for work at a different level. The quantifiable part is essential, even though it brings a different flavor to the conversation.

To help you make goal setting the centerpiece of your coaching experience, here are five ways you can maintain that focus on measurability.

## Let Employees Participate in the Goal-Setting Process

If coaches just set goals without input, employees may find it harder to commit to reaching them. The lack of control might even increase the negative sense of pressure they experience.

On the other hand, if employees are involved in every aspect of goal setting, they automatically feel a greater sense of responsibility for meeting those goals. They are more engaged when they participate in determining what's possible—such as setting interim deadlines and progressive objectives—for the short term, for the long term, and over the span of their careers.

## Connect Individual Goals to the Organization's Goals

One of the best ways to guide employees in setting (and even exceeding) goals is by linking those directly to the company's goals. Whatever they set out to do needs to make sense from a big-picture perspective. Here are some examples of how to connect their work with corporate outcomes:

> "During our annual review, we committed to making sure our new employees—in office and virtual—feel properly onboarded and welcomed in their new roles. What kind of intentional efforts are you prepared to make to help meet that commitment?"

> "The company set some ambitious goals for growth this quarter. If you add four new customers in that time frame, you increase corporate revenue by 8 percent."

Employees want to feel like they have a purpose—like what they do really matters and they have the power to make a difference on a larger scale. And science proves it. Otherwise, it feels irrelevant and unnecessary. Help them make that connection.

## Secure a Commitment

Talking about a goal isn't the same thing as making the promise to achieve it. As a coach, it's your job to make sure the goals are actionable and measurable with a timeline attached. More specifically, be sure your employees understand the full scope of the plan and "buy in."

Be deliberate about letting them take ownership of the process. Ask questions like, "So what are we committing to here?" By bouncing the ball back into their court, you're allowing them to take control. Even better, you're securing an emotional commitment and laying the groundwork for their accountability.

## Keep the Commitment Alive

It's tempting as a coach to finish the goal-setting part of the process and then leave things on the back burner until the next review. That, however, undermines the benefits of the coaching relationship. To be effective, coaches need to pay close attention to employees' progress.

Have check-ins to see are they on track. Are they off by a mile? What's getting in the way?

Always knowing the quantifiable "score" as the year progresses allows coaches to customize conversations with employees. In real time, coaches can help employees learn skills they can apply to whatever challenge they are currently facing and to see the impact on their performance. With this kind of just-in-time coaching, employees get the specific support they need in the moment and the immediate results to go with it.

## Remain Flexible with Your Coaching Goals

Situations change and new opportunities emerge. As the coach, you determine with your employees when it might be sensible or even necessary to adjust their goals.

Rigid adherence to goals that, for whatever reason, have become unrealistic and unobtainable since originally set will only create stress and anxiety for everyone involved. On the other hand, if the people you are coaching have blown past the initial goals eight months into the year, revisit those to continue keeping them challenged.

Changing goals should be a collaborative decision. You definitely want discussion and buy-in during that process. Otherwise your employees will feel like they are constantly chasing a moving target. The point here? Remain flexible.

When you take a positive and strategic approach to goal setting as you coach your employees, you can transform the way they think about their commitment to the organization. In addition, you can dramatically increase their engagement and performance, as well as their potential to contribute at a higher level throughout their careers.

• • •

When you work to incorporate these foundational skills, you will make huge strides in your quest to become a more effective coach. Rapport-building sets the all-important tone. Asking strategic questions without judgment and actively listening will arm you with valuable information. Providing rich feedback and pushing your coachees out of their comfort zones can give them the fuel they need to be successful and reach the concrete goals you have set together.

If you are consistent with layering and reinforcing these coaching skills, you will reap the benefits.

## ESSENTIAL TAKEAWAYS

- Build trust and rapport as a starting point or your coaching is likely to be less effective.

- Come to the table with others' best interests at heart—not with the goal to find the fastest, easiest solution.

- Get to genuinely and deeply know the people you coach by listening to, engaging with, and supporting them.

- Use questions strategically to uncover a higher quality of information that will elevate your coaching.

- Improve your impact as a coach by paying close attention to your communication style and actively listen with intent.

- Gather feedback on your coaching skills to help improve self-awareness and make sure your intent matches your impact on others.

- Remember to take feedback purposefully, not personally— and encourage your coachees to do the same.

CHAPTER

4

# Attributes of a
# Great Coach

**Some people think coaching** is a job reserved only for outgoing and charismatic people, counselor-types, or those who have led some sort of sports team. That's just not true. With the right skills and a genuine desire to succeed, *anyone* can be a good coach.

With that said, I would be remiss if I didn't point out that there's also an intangible side to the equation. That "coaching X factor." The secret sauce. Great coaching comes down to more than *what* coaches do. It's also about *how* they do it. I'm referring to a set of characteristics that the most successful coaches tend to have in common. Not in a cookie-cutter kind of way. Just some interesting similarities in their mindsets and demeanors.

That may leave you wondering if you have what it takes to be an effective coach. The short answer? Yes! And I know that because you've already picked up this book.

Regardless of your innate personality and experiences, you can become an outstanding coach by paying close attention to the way you apply the skills and techniques you've learned so far. Plus, without changing who you are, you can work toward adopting the attributes that tend to elevate good leaders into great coaches.

For each of these characteristics, we'll first take a closer look at what they mean in the context of coaching. Then you'll work through some actionable strategies you can use—starting today—to incorporate these attributes into your leadership brand.

Remember that it will take some time for all of these characteristics to seep in and become a natural part of your coaching persona. Let's start that journey with some basic steps to begin moving you in the right direction. These targeted, cut-to-the-chase suggestions will help give you the momentum you need. After all, getting started is 51 percent of the battle, right?

So, let's get to it.

## EMOTIONALLY INTELLIGENT

Emotional intelligence is defined by the *Oxford English Dictionary* as "the capacity to be aware of, control, and express one's emotions, and to handle interpersonal relationships judiciously and empathetically." Popularized by American psychologist Daniel Goleman in 1995, this discipline has become an increasingly important skill to have in the business world. According to Goleman, there are five key elements that make up emotional intelligence: self-awareness, self-regulation, motivation, empathy, and social skills.

Without a doubt, high emotional intelligence is a signature ingredient found in the most successful coaches. These leaders understand not just their own strengths and weaknesses, but also how their temperaments and belief systems impact their coaching process. They recognize how their emotions can influence their interactions with others, and they work hard to manage those. They know how to read the room and determine whether they are having the impact on others that they intend. Even better, they pivot and make real-time adjustments to improve that impact. In the coaching environment, that can be particularly powerful.

Coaches who are self-aware also realize that they are still (and always will be) a work in progress. They have their own development goals and consistently seek out new opportunities to learn.

## How to Get Started: Boosting Your Emotional Intelligence

Many people believe emotional intelligence is just as important as cognitive intelligence. Here's the difference: Our cognitive intelligence is relatively fixed throughout our lifetimes, but we have the power to increase our emotional intelligence. Although the capacity differs from person to person, it's a skill that can be learned and developed. The strategies that follow can help you become more emotionally intelligent.

### *Set Aside Time to Practice Self-Reflection*
Think about your coaching interactions with others (in person, virtually, on the phone, through email, via text), and think about some questions:

- *Did your interactions today go the way you hoped they would? If not, what may have gone wrong?*

- *Did you remove all distractions so you could be fully present with your coachee?*

- *Did your emotions, temperament, beliefs, and past experiences influence your decision-making as a coach in a positive or negative way?*

- *How do you want the people you coach to see and experience you?*

### *Improve Your Self-Awareness by Intentionally Seeking Feedback from Others*

To know for sure how others are experiencing you as a coach, ask. Rather than just asking, "Hey, how am I doing as a coach?" (which is likely to elicit an automatic response of "Great!"), get specific with your questions. For instance: "My goal is to be seen as a coach who is patient, creative, and supportive. Is there anything I'm doing that either contributes to or detracts from that perception?" The important thing is to find out whether others are experiencing you the way you intended. If you find a gap between your intent and your actual impact, identify some simple ways to shift your approach so you can better engage and influence the people around you.

Perhaps you discover that your coachees see you as patient but not necessarily creative. How could you shake things up in future coaching conversations? Consider reaching out to your peers to get fresh ideas on how to help your coachees sharpen specific skills or introduce new ways of sharing information so that it sparks innovating thinking. You can use the feedback you gather to make subtle changes that add up over time and increase your impact as a coach. Emotional intelligence fuels those important shifts.

## *Be Deliberate About Managing Your Emotions and Controlling Your Impulses*

This doesn't mean you should adopt a robotic approach that eliminates all traces of smiles, frowns, and stress. You're still human! But great coaches know how to establish and maintain their credibility by monitoring their words, reactions, facial expressions, and body language. Instead of verbally and visibly broadcasting your opinions about something, you may be more effective as a coach if you maintain an image of neutrality and let your employees come to their own conclusions.

With our current climate of constant change and unpredictable circumstances, it's not easy to remain calm and in control at all times. But keep in mind that your coachees look to you as a role model for how to handle difficult situations—even if you're not in the middle of a coaching session. They are learning how to be a better leader by watching you navigate the choppy waters of uncertainty, so make sure to set a good example.

One suggestion for improving impulse control is to create some space between your ego and your mind. This space allows you to pause and let your rational mind catch up with your emotional mind. It's like the seven-second delay in a broadcast: A little space prevents impulsiveness from taking over.

Think before you speak. Think before you act. Think before your eyes inadvertently share what your brain is screaming. (Yes, there's an unmistakable look that communicates "are you absolutely insane?" with a single glance, so it's best to avoid that!) If you want to be an effective and emotionally intelligent coach, work on becoming more poised and composed even when under pressure.

*Flex Your Empathy Muscle*

To increase your emotional intelligence, actively work to understand the thoughts and feelings of the people you coach. Before you jump in with the "obvious" solution or direction, force yourself to stop and think. What are the circumstances and challenges facing this employee? What's driving the way this person is approaching the situation? What past experiences are at play in his or her decision-making on this project? If you don't know the answers, find out. The goal is to put yourself in that person's shoes and see tasks through that person's eyes.

When you make it a habit to infuse your coaching conversations with a healthy dose of empathy, you're more likely to generate positive results: strengthening trust, reinforcing your sense of partnership, inspiring your coachees, and occasionally uncovering solutions you hadn't previously considered.

## FULLY PRESENT

Another trademark of great coaches is the ability to give employees their complete attention during coaching sessions. On the surface that doesn't sound like an outrageous demand, but the potential distractions in today's world (physical, mental, digital, and emotional) can be overwhelming.

It can be hard to fully focus on the person in front of us if we are preoccupied, bored, stressed, waiting for a text, wondering about the basketball score, anticipating an important phone call . . . you name it. And we all know what it's like to be with people who are physically (or virtually) present while their minds are somewhere else. That speaks volumes about how we rank in the priority list of their relationships and tasks.

Now apply that concept to a coaching situation. If you want to build trust and establish true partnerships with the people you coach, you have to be deliberate about blocking out the urgent deadlines and the chaos swirling around you so you can stay fully present. That kind of focus also allows you to organize your thoughts and communicate effectively rather than delivering scattered explanations or vague strategies. It's impossible to guide someone in a logical and meaningful way if distractions have hijacked your brain.

## How to Get Started: Being More Present

Being fully present requires practice, but I want to share a few tips to help you achieve your goal of remaining in the "here and now" as you coach your employees.

### Build in Some Buffer Time Before Your Coaching Sessions

Make sure that your other tasks and meetings end well before your coaching sessions begin. That will give you time to get some closure from those activities and jot down any notes or follow-up reminders before you shift gears. Spend a few minutes intentionally decompressing and preparing for the session before your coachee arrives. If you discover any nagging thoughts racing through your brain, write them down so you can temporarily let them go.

### Remove Distractions

This one is simple but highly effective. Choose a location for the conversation that minimizes noise and potential interruptions. Silence your digital devices (seriously . . . all of them). Put your phone away so you won't be tempted to divert your attention when you get alerts or pop-up notifications. If you're in your office, remove papers and reports from your desk area and close the door if possible.

### Be Deliberate About Plugging In

The first two tips set the stage for being fully present, but this is where the rubber meets the road. Once the coaching conversation starts, show that you are an active participant in the session. Make natural eye contact. Listen carefully. Lean forward slightly and nod when appropriate. The other way to demonstrate your attentiveness is by making strategic comments including:

- **Asking questions:** "What do you think you might do differently next time?"

- **Validating their feelings:** "That must have been very frustrating for you."

- **Paraphrasing their comments:** "So it sounds like you are saying we really need to choose a different vendor if we want to meet the deadline. Is that correct?"

## IMPARTIAL AND FAIR

I've mentioned it before, but it bears repeating: Great coaches aren't judgmental, and they don't enter coaching relationships with their own natural bias. No taking sides. No underlying assumptions that their own opinions are the correct view of any issue. They remain objective and deliberately set aside any personal agendas.

Beyond being impartial and fair, they are also open-minded. They welcome diversity of thought, even when it runs counter to their own ideas. That willingness to listen and understand different points of view can make a strong impression on employees who are beginning to stretch their own thinking. It allows these coachees to feel comfortable establishing their own identities rather than feeling the pressure to parrot whatever stance their coaches deem appropriate or the gold standard of responses.

## How to Get Started: Becoming More Impartial and Fair

Taking a stance of neutrality might be one of the most important attributes when it comes to being an effective coach. Following are a few ways to move toward that goal.

### *Seek Out the Facts*

Weed out any judgmental slant on situations, ideas, and decisions by evaluating factual information related to your coachees. That includes everything from performance reports to sales figures and even customer satisfaction ratings. And yes, sometimes your own observations need to be factored in as well. What went wrong in that situation? What was the real impetus behind such an amazing success? What might be preventing this person from reaching their potential?

In those cases where your educated opinions become part of the landscape, analyze the circumstances without assuming intent or assigning emotions. When you can launch conversations from a fact-based foundation, you and your coachee are more likely to agree on that baseline before moving forward. That creates an atmosphere of trust and a sense that the two of you are coming together to meet a common goal.

### Share Your Rationale

A little transparency goes a long way when it comes to coaching. From the beginning, make sure the people you coach understand the "why" behind your conversations. When you share an opinion, clearly support your viewpoint with logical explanations. And as you reach decisions together, make sure your coachee fully understands the purpose behind the choices made.

Here's why that is so important. If the people you coach don't understand your rationale, they may not fully buy in to the direction and choices made during a coaching conversation. Their imaginations and thoughts begin to churn—and not in a good way: *Why would he recommend that when it doesn't seem to fit with what we've done before? Is there a hidden agenda here?*

Avoid that doubt and uncertainty by filling in the blanks. When people know the reasons behind the choices, they can better process them and determine whether they consider any actions to be fair and neutral. If they are left to guess, they may attach subjective intent that leads to an erosion of trust.

### Hold All of Your Employees to the Same Standards

This is a big one, so make a mental note of it. No matter how hard you try to sound fair and impartial in your coaching conversations, that perception will evaporate if you don't apply the same performance and behavioral standards for *all* of your employees. This isn't about having a rigid demeanor but being consistently fair about consequences and rewards for your whole team. If your top-performing employee and the team slacker miss a deadline, they should both be held accountable for their actions in equal measure.

On a related note, be sure to model these consistent standards and show that you practice what you preach. Is punctuality something you expect from your team? Don't show up 20 minutes late to a meeting with a Starbucks cup and a croissant as if you're exempt from the rules. Show your coachees that the standards apply not only to them, but also to you, your peers, and even your supervisor.

## INSATIABLY CURIOUS

Outstanding coaches have a natural curiosity that leads them to want more information about situations that intrigue or concern them. They search for possibilities that others might overlook. Once their interest is sparked, they remain focused to get more details or to find out the why behind something. As noted in Chapter 3, great coaches use rich and open-ended questions not just to satisfy their curiosity, but also to solicit the perspectives of those they coach and ultimately to guide them in the right direction.

### How to Get Started: Increasing Your Curiosity

There are a number of things you can do to ignite your curiosity. The tips that follow are designed to help you expand your inquisitive and creative sides.

#### Adopt the Mantra, "What If . . . ?"
As a general rule, push yourself to think about processes, decisions, and strategies from a fresh perspective—especially the ones that have slipped into autopilot mode. What if you tried a different approach? What if you stopped generating that report nobody reads? What if you hit pause and searched for feedback from someone who will likely try to talk you out of what you're planning to do? Start asking more

questions that buck the status quo and open the door for novel ways of thinking and doing.

### Cast Your Net Wider

If you're like most people, you tend to read the same publications, listen to the same podcasts, or watch the same TV programs every week. It's time to knock your way through those mental boundaries!

Find something unexpected to supplement your usual sources of information. Perhaps follow someone new on LinkedIn or Twitter. What fresh information, perspectives, and opinions can you gather? Maybe it's not even business-related—such as exotic travel destinations, sustainable gardening, or wearable technology. Whatever it is, make a commitment to learn more about something that piques your interest and gets your brain in the habit of searching for more information. That's how curiosity takes root and, hopefully, starts to bloom in your coaching conversations.

### Create a Culture of Curiosity

As a coach, you can begin to demonstrate what it looks like to employ curiosity as a leadership tool. Set the example by asking smart questions: "Why have we always done it this way?" "Does it still make sense?" "What do you think would happen if we flip that idea on its head?" As you build your sense of curiosity, you can simultaneously pass that along to your coachees and team members.

Establish some ground rules: No question is a stupid question. Encourage them to be inquisitive and make it safe for them to push the boundaries. When the people you coach know that you're a champion for continuous learning and sharing knowledge (inside and outside of your team), they will begin to adopt the same attitude and establish a culture of curiosity.

# INSIGHTFUL AND PERCEPTIVE

Leader-coaches help their employees to grow by sharing the fruits of their experiences. They know how to put things in context and provide a broader perspective. Sometimes that insight involves a reminder that a mistake isn't the end of the world. Other times, it's a gentle push to help them stretch their thinking and see even greater opportunities on the horizon. When coaches can perceptively guide their employees to view challenges through a wider lens, they can shorten the learning curve and accelerate development.

## How to Get Started: Becoming More Perceptive

Coaches who are considered perceptive and insightful have a knack for reading between the lines and seeing things that a less seasoned professional might not catch. Try the following tips to strengthen that characteristic.

### *Work to Become a Master Observer*
Start paying closer attention to the nuances in the people around you, especially during your coaching sessions or when you are observing one of your coachees at work. What are their facial expressions and body language telling you that doesn't come through in their words or actions? Use that information to gain a better understanding of their thoughts, feelings, and values. Then extrapolate to determine whether any of those elements are having an impact on their work or your coaching conversation.

### *Leverage Your Experience and Intuition*
Considering your own industry knowledge and the trends you've seen throughout your career, you may have insights that could help predict

the outcomes of certain choices or decisions made by your coachees. How can you share that experience-based intuition and the longer-term perspectives to benefit the people you coach? The key is to add those insights without squelching their creativity or innovative approaches.

## GENUINELY AFFIRMING

The most successful coaches enter each coaching relationship with a sense of optimism and an expectation that good outcomes are possible. They honestly believe that the people they coach, regardless of organizational status or position, have the potential to develop beyond their current skills and responsibilities.

### How to Get Started: Affirming Others

When your coachees trust you, they will begin to get comfortable showing more vulnerability or even doubt. If you want to reward that openness and strengthen the relationship, provide emotional support with some positive affirmations. Need a few ideas?

*Point Out Their Strengths Regularly*
In your conversations, make an effort to use statements that acknowledge the characteristics and behaviors that are leading to their progressive success. Show that you recognize and appreciate the things they are doing well and the areas where they are shining. Those comments will increase their confidence and help them build on their natural abilities. For instance:

- "You are clearly a subject matter expert on this topic."

- "You handled that tense moment exceptionally well."

- "That's a fantastic suggestion."

### Believe in the Potential of Those You Coach

Don't be afraid to nudge your coachees out of their comfort zones when you know they can achieve more. Tell them straight out that you believe in them and their capacity for doing great things. Then give them stretch goals, be vocal about your confidence in their abilities along the way, and make sure they know you will support them—even if they fail.

### Celebrate Their Successes

When your coachees achieve a milestone or a big "win," join them in the excitement. Be generous with praise and show your enthusiasm about their accomplishments. Their success is your success, so let them know you are sharing in the celebration.

## PATIENT AND COMPOSED

Smart coaches understand that growth takes time, and they don't expect everything to fall into place according to their own schedules. They know how to move their coachees forward at the right pace—not too fast or too slow. They also follow the wisdom of the famous adage: *Give a man a fish, and you feed him for a day. Teach a man to fish, and you feed him for a lifetime.* In other words, smart leaders provide direction while allowing their coachees to solve problems on their own so they're better prepared for the future.

That kind of patience is also essential for leaders when the people they coach make errors or bad decisions. Experienced coaches don't get rattled when things go wrong. Instead, they maintain a polished sense of professionalism and help to bring an even keel to situations, even when others are flustered.

## How to Get Started: Improving Your Patience

Some people work on this attribute for a lifetime, so cut yourself some slack if you don't magically transform your demeanor after reading the suggestions that follow.

### *Remind Yourself That Coaching Isn't Always a Linear Process*

No matter how effective you are, things may evolve in a two-steps-forward-one-step-back manner. Accept that and try to release any unrealistic expectations that may be causing you frustration.

Along the same lines, there will never be a single formula that works with every person you coach. If your coachee seems to be stuck, rethink the situation and consider following a different direction. And even when things aren't falling into place as you originally envisioned, stay focused on the ultimate goal and realize that your coachee will benefit from the journey as much as the destination.

### *Let Go of Rigid Timelines for Development*

While projects may come with specific deadlines, developmental growth may follow its own clock. Keep in mind that everyone's appetite for change and capacity for incorporating new approaches may be different. Step back and meet people wherever they are, recognizing they are unique individuals. Remind yourself that it's important to allow your coachees' development to progress at its own pace.

### Schedule Coaching Sessions
### When You Are at Your Best

We all have times during the day when our patience is in more abundance than others. If you're a morning person, schedule your coaching sessions before noon. If you are perpetually grumpy on Monday afternoons after all the budget reports are due, that's not a great time to inspire and motivate others. You'll always be more effective if you coach when your patience is at its peak.

### Adopt Practices That Help You Manage Your Stress

Life can be complicated, and coaching certainly isn't the only potential source of stress in your days. Prioritize your own mental health by making exercise, yoga, or meditation part of your regular routine. These activities will help you build resilience and give you a much-needed outlet for your stress so you don't "unload" on your coachees or your coworkers.

## KIND AND CONSIDERATE

The best leaders approach coaching relationships as caring partnerships. They consistently treat those they coach with kindness and respect, and they work hard to develop trust. They can be honest and transparent without using language that might sound condescending or abrupt. They even approach their coaching interactions with a sense of humility and recognize they can learn something new from each coachee.

## How to Get Started:
## Boosting Your Kindness Quotient

Whether you are coaching an employee or handling a sticky situation with a neighbor, you can never go wrong if you err on the side of more kindness. These suggestions can help you become a more polite and courteous coach.

### *Choose Your Words Carefully: They Matter!*

As your relationships with your coachees grow, you may have a tendency to become more casual in your interactions. Just don't assume that gives you permission to drop the niceties of conversations that keep them cordial. If you have a request, ask politely. Limit words like "you will" or "obviously" or "don't" that may sound overly demanding. And if your coachees make a contribution to the team, be sure to express your gratitude and appreciation.

Sometimes you'll have to share negative information with the people you coach. It's inevitable. But *how* you go about sharing that information is critical.

If you embark on those conversations with the heavy use of the word "you," your coachees may interpret it as blame or judgment. That creates an uncomfortable setting for both of you. Instead, pause to imagine how you might receive feedback about a disappointing outcome and "package" your words with an extra layer of kindness. Note the differences in these examples:

- "*You* did this" versus "This is what *I* observed."

- "*You* shouldn't have done that" versus "Here's how *I* think that might have been perceived."

- "*You* must be crazy" versus "*I'd* like to talk more about the ramifications of that choice."

### *Monitor Your Tone*

Even if you have the best of intentions and carefully choose your words, be cognizant of your tone of voice. Is it in alignment with what you're saying, or is it telling another story? If you're trying to create a safe space for your coachee to speak candidly but you sound rushed and irritable, your tone trumps your words. Ask yourself before (and during) every coaching session: *Am I being compassionately candid and genuinely supportive? Can my employees hear that kindness in my voice as well as my actual words?*

*Show Some Grace*

Every person you coach is a busy and fallible human being. Perfection isn't in the cards, no matter how spectacular your coaching skills might be. Recognize that your employees have lives outside of the office, and they may be dealing with stressors and concerns you know nothing about. When mistakes happen (and they will), always make kindness a go-to resource when you respond.

# GROWTH MINDED

Leaders who personally aspire to develop with each new experience and aim to evolve their ideas and beliefs are considered to have a growth mindset. These same leaders embrace the idea of "the beginner's mind." Originating from the word "Shoshin" in Zen Buddhism, this concept refers to the ability to drop all the assumptions we bring to tasks and situations we have encountered many times. When we see things through the eyes of a beginner, we can imagine more possibilities. It's like trading in a cynical view ("That will never work!") for an optimistic, ambitious outlook ("Let's find a way to make it work!").

This is critical on a number of different levels. Growth-minded leaders have a greater chance of cultivating that type of mindset in the people they coach. When coachees see that their role models are demonstrating openness to feedback, welcoming new ideas, and learning from their mistakes, they tend to follow that example—increasing their curiosity, becoming more flexible, and remaining open to continuous learning and development.

## How to Get Started: Becoming More Growth Minded

Here are four action items to help you demonstrate your commitment to growth and development in a way that inspires your coachees to do the same.

### Take on New Challenges

Instead of allowing yourself to get complacent, push yourself to tackle new challenges—and don't be afraid to share with your coachees that it can be an uncomfortable process at times. That helps them realize that it's perfectly normal to feel the fear, but it's also possible to find the courage to move past it at the same time. Part of developing a growth mindset is embracing new experiences and accepting that you may not perform at your usual speed early on.

### Get Hooked on Learning

Establish your own plans for growth and development. Be deliberate about how you choose to improve your skills and learn new things, and make it an ongoing process. Does that mean going back to school for an advanced degree or getting a new certification? Would you gain more knowledge by participating in a special project or volunteering to lead a committee within your trade organization? What skills do you need to make you better at what you do? Figure that out and determine the shortest path to get there. Your coachees will be watching.

### Ask for Feedback

Your professional growth doesn't need to occur in a vacuum. As you work to develop your own skills, seek input from trusted advisors, peers, leaders, and even friends. Find out if they have a different perspective or some helpful insights that could accelerate your pace of growth. Get their advice to help you learn from your mistakes. And, an area sometimes overlooked, ask for their opinions about the priority of learning new skills in terms of impact for short- and long-term horizons.

### Demonstrate the Power of Continuous Growth

As a coach, you can model what it means to value learning over perfection. That shows your employees that it's more important to be a work in progress when it comes to growth rather than constantly trying to prove that you're the smartest person in the room.

Developmental momentum should be a nonstop adventure—for you *and* your coachees. Be open about sharing your journey of growth and the rewards that come with it. And when the people you coach take the initiative to improve their own development, become their biggest advocate.

## DISCREET

The ability to maintain confidentiality is a huge part of being a respected and admired coach. In fact, great coaches work hard to establish relationships and create coaching conversations in which employees feel comfortable enough to share sensitive information. The quickest way to ruin that trust (and undermine the impact of your coaching) is to pass along any details shared in confidence.

Some people find it helpful to draw the parallel of coaching conversations with the concept of attorney/client privilege in their favorite legal dramas. Take it seriously. Be discreet. Whatever they tell you stays "in the vault." Period.

## How to Get Started: Strengthening Your Discretion

Your reputation as a coach and a leader will be determined by how well you can hold information in confidence. The follow guidelines can help you become more airtight with comments made during your coaching conversations.

### *Set Ground Rules at the Beginning of the Coaching Relationship*

State your intent regarding confidentiality in your first coaching conversation. Share your thoughts about boundaries and ask your coachee to do the same. Having that discussion from the beginning will help avoid any misunderstandings and make those you coach feel more comfortable with sharing.

### *Stick to the Plan*

It's simultaneously simple and yet incredibly difficult to never share information from a private coaching conversation unless the two of you have specifically agreed to that in advance. Building trust is the hallmark of a great coaching relationship, and nothing can erode that faster than someone finding out you disclosed information meant to be kept private.

### *Be Diligent About Your Record-Keeping*

If you take notes during your coaching conversations, be vigilant about how you store them. Are your records safe in printed or digital form? Who might possibly have access to them? How long do you keep them? It's important to protect that information, especially when you've been coaching someone who asked for sound advice on handling a sticky situation or needed help navigating some internal politics.

### *Get Permission If Things Change*

In the event that you need to disclose a certain type of information from a coaching conversation, get permission from your employee before you do so. Let them know in advance what you are sharing, with whom, and why. Then stay focused on minimizing the disclosures, only providing information that is necessary and relevant.

• • •

If you can be intentional about incorporating these characteristics in your demeanor as a leader-coach, you'll quickly see the results in the quality of your coaching relationships. You still need to master the foundational skills involved, but folding in these intangible attributes has an almost uncanny way of elevating the impact of every coaching interaction. The individual nuances may be hard to isolate, but the cumulative effect is powerful.

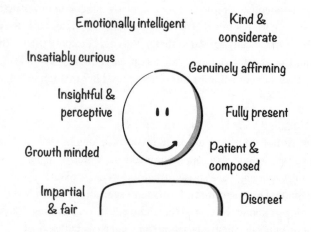

The main point bears repeating. Great coaching isn't just about *what* you do but also *how* you do it. And when you coach from a place of kindness, patience, fairness, curiosity, attentiveness, and optimism, the odds of success are overwhelmingly in your favor.

## ESSENTIAL TAKEAWAYS

- Great coaching comes down to more than *what* you do. It's also about *how* you do it.

- The attributes of a great coach include being emotionally intelligent, fully present, impartial and fair, insatiably curious, insightful and perceptive, genuinely affirming, patient and composed, kind and considerate, growth minded, and discreet.

- When coaches demonstrate openness to feedback, new ideas, and learning from their mistakes, the people they coach tend to follow that example—increasing their curiosity, becoming more flexible, and remaining open to continuous learning and development.

**CHAPTER**

**5**

# Knowledge Check

**As we wrap up** Part I on the essentials of coaching, it's time to test your knowledge. Take a moment to answer the questions below and jot down any related ideas for reference. (Feel free to revisit earlier chapters as needed, and you'll find the Answer Key for the Chapter 5 Knowledge Check at the back of this book.) The goal of this Knowledge Check is to ensure that you have a solid grasp of the basic components before we move on to talk about coaching applications.

1. **Leadership coaching has proven benefits for:**

   a. The person being coached

   b. The leader

   c. The company

   d. All of the above

2. What's the connection between being an effective coach and being a successful leader? What potential results link those two roles?

3. The two main types of coaching include _____ and _____. Thinking about the people currently on your team, which type of coaching do they need most from you right now? What are the advantages of providing both types?

4. What are the five steps in the coaching framework?

5. What are some different ways you can provide support for the people you coach?

6. Why are building trust and developing rapport critical as the first steps in coaching?

7. **Which of the statements below are examples of open-ended questions?**

    a. How are you today?

    b. What did you do this weekend?

    c. Are you on track to meet the deadline?

    d. What's happening with the project this week?

    e. Did the meeting go well?

    f. What factors contributed to the lively discussion at the meeting?

8. **Listening is one of the most important skills for effective coaches. What are some of the listening skills you can use with your coachees?**

9. **Think of a time in a coaching session when you may not have suspended judgment or assumed positive intent. What was the outcome? Looking back, what, if anything, would you have changed about that interaction?**

10. **Great coaches know how to give great feedback. What are the five ways they can do this?**

11. Name a few ways you can let your employees drive the discussion versus you taking the lead.

12. Write down as many words or phrases as you can to describe the attributes of a great coach.

13. Select one of the attributes you listed above and describe what that looks like "in action" during a coaching session.

## PART II

# THE ESSENTIALS APPLIED

# Coaching Self-Assessment

Now that you *understand* the essentials, you're ready to *apply* the essentials. To get started, complete the benchmark assessment below. Your answers will help to highlight the areas you can target in Part II to make the most dramatic improvement in your coaching skills. No one else needs to see this, so feel free to be brutally honest. You'll have a chance to complete this assessment again later to document your progress.

***Directions:*** Please read each statement and use the following scale to indicate how strongly you agree with it. Then add up the rating column for a total score at the bottom.

1 = Never
2 = Rarely
3 = Sometimes
4 = Usually
5 = Always

| Rating | |
|---|---|
| | When coaching employees, I assume positive intent. |
| | I keep an open mind and try to understand the point of view of others. |
| | When coaching employees, I show genuine curiosity in what they have to say. |
| | I ask probing and open-ended questions to better understand a situation before giving my advice. |

| | |
|---|---|
| | When I listen, I try to clarify what my employees have said by summarizing what I heard. |
| | When listening, I give my full attention and put all distractions aside. |
| | I demonstrate attentiveness with eye contact and body language. |
| | I provide positive and negative feedback in a timely manner. |
| | I help employees recognize their strengths and areas for improvement. |
| | I help employees understand the impact of their behavior. |
| | I help employees identify any potential misalignment between their intended impact and how others actually experience them. |
| | I give my employees the benefit of the doubt. |
| | I take time to understand the long-term career aspirations of the people I coach. |
| | I encourage my employees to challenge their own assumptions and explore new ideas/approaches. |
| | I help employees come up with their own solutions rather than imposing mine. |
| | I support my employees in identifying goals that will have the most impact on their success at work. |

| | |
|---|---|
| | I partner with my employees to create development plans that will help them become more effective in reaching their immediate goals. |
| | I partner with my employees to create development plans targeted to prepare them for career advancement. |
| | I believe that I genuinely share in the success of those I coach. |
| | I offer continuous support, encouragement, and accountability as part of my coaching practice. |
| | **Maximum Score: 100** |

Add up your total score to determine your percentage of the 100 possible points. This score is only the "starting line"—a way to help measure your progress as you learn more about coaching applications in this Part, "The Essentials Applied." Once you've had a chance to practice new coaching strategies, repeat this assessment to track your growth.

Right now, this benchmark assessment can also help you gain some valuable insights into your specific coaching skill levels. Any statements that you ranked as a 4 or a 5 may represent your strengths as a coach. Statements that you ranked as 1, 2, or 3 provide you with opportunities for improvement.

Circle or highlight the three to five statements with the lowest scores. As you work through Part II and begin to practice some of your coaching skills in real time, pay close attention to those specific areas. If you focus on accelerating those particular skills, you'll likely see the biggest change in your coaching performance and results.

CHAPTER

6

# Performance Coaching in Action

**This chapter and the** next will give you a chance to start incorporating the knowledge you've gained about coaching so you can make the shift from theory to application. In this chapter, you'll see Performance Coaching in action, and in the next, you'll take a dive deeper into Developmental Coaching. The good news is you can begin building your mental coaching muscles before you actually have to use them with a direct report.

To launch that transition, we'll borrow a tactic often used in the world of football. While the players on the field are getting in their "physical reps," the players standing on the sidelines are getting in their "mental reps." This involves analyzing plays from a strategic viewpoint and thinking through how they would handle each scenario as it unfolds. The more they practice that real-time analysis, the easier it is to translate those thought processes into deliberate actions on the field. And, with enough repetition, muscle memory kicks in. That type of strategic thinking becomes instinct.

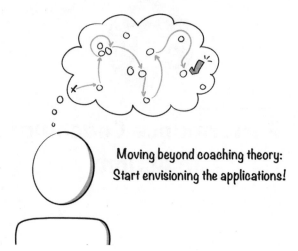

Moving beyond coaching theory:
Start envisioning the applications!

That's exactly what this chapter will do. It provides you with some opportunities to get in mental reps that will build your coaching instincts. Each example will begin with details about a hypothetical coaching scenario that might be found in a real-world business environment, followed by some prompts to help you think through the strategy you might use.

I strongly encourage you to spend some time considering your approach and jotting down your answers to the questions before you move on. (Seriously, don't skip this step. You'll thank me later.) At the end of each section, you'll also find sample dialogue to show how this particular challenge might translate into a successful coaching session.

Let's start with some examples of Performance Coaching designed to help employees become more effective in their current jobs, specifically closing skill gaps, correcting behavior problems, clarifying expectations, and discussing accountability.

## COACHING FOSTER:
## LEARNING TO VALUE INPUT FROM OTHERS

Foster is known in your company as a high-tech guru. He lives and breathes technology. Incredibly intelligent, visionary, and experienced, he has been reporting to you for just over a year.

The problem? Foster's drive for perfection and performance has diminished his reputation and negatively impacted his ability to form strong working relationships. He is very independent and doesn't seem to enjoy collaboration. You're hearing that his colleagues find him elusive (or worse) and no longer include him in team meet-ups. No amount of brilliance can compensate for the perception that Foster isn't a team player and has no interest in the contributions and perspectives of others.

### Getting Started

You asked Foster to meet with you this afternoon, and you go into this conversation hopeful that he will be open to making some changes. Before he arrives in your office, think about the strategy you will use to address these performance issues. Record your answers in the spaces below:

- How can you point out areas for improvement while also reassuring Foster that his expertise is important and valued?

- How can you help Foster understand the value of collaboration?

- What steps do you think would help him to begin making meaningful changes?

- What advice and support should you offer to Foster?

You begin this session by saying, "Hello, Foster! Thanks for taking the time to visit with me. Catch me up on how things are going with you." And, then you go into each of the five steps of coaching.

## Step 1: Assess the Situation

**Foster:** "Sure! Remember I told you I was doing an analysis on our new network? Well, I found some problems. It wasn't properly optimized. In fact, I wouldn't even consider it stable. I completely reworked the whole thing, and now it is in top shape. So much better, I can't even tell you. I got a little pushback afterward from the people who originally set it up, but I think I convinced them why we needed to make the changes."

**You:** "Sounds like you've been busy. How do you think things are going with the other people on your team?"

**Foster:** "Ha! Let's just say it's not great right now. Some of them were involved in the transition to the network, so I think they may have been offended by my improvements. But seriously, how could they have thought that thing was robust? I didn't want to open a whole can of worms with a big discussion about the problems. It was just easier for me to fix it myself rather than try to explain it all to them."

**You:** "I hear what you're saying, but I also think there's a benefit to using your expertise in a way that helps your team and your coworkers learn. Technology aside, how do you view your role as a team lead?"

**Foster:** "Hmm . . . I guess I think of myself more as a manager of technology than a manager of people. I mean, yeah, they report to me, but that's just because I have more experience with the IT systems."

## Step 2: Generate Ideas

**You:** "Well, let's talk about that. The leadership side is actually an important part of your position. I know you've told me in the past that you want to grow with the company and eventually take on more responsibility. Engaging your team and valuing their experience and input are critical parts of that puzzle. Along that line, I've gotten some feedback that you seem to make decisions without getting any input. What can you tell me about that?"

**Foster:** "You know, I get busy. I know exactly what needs to happen with the network. I don't need a bunch of meetings and emails to figure it out. I just get it done. That's why you hired me!"

**You:** "That's *part* of why you were hired. Have you ever considered that there might be something you could gain from those meetings and emails? Maybe someone on your team remembers how a technology decision a few years ago had a negative impact on another department. That's important information to know. Or somebody else could describe a huge e-commerce site that recently failed because of some crazy reason no one would have guessed. That conversation could mean you make a mental note and avoid that mistake in the future. Those different perspectives and experiences all come together and indirectly add value to what you are already doing so well."

**Foster:** "Yeah, I guess I can see that. It's not like they're trying to tell me how to do my job. They are just giving me information that could help me do it better."

**You:** "Exactly. I think you have a lot of potential to expand your influence in the organization. But what do you think might hold you back from that, based on our conversation today?"

**Foster:** "Hmmm . . . I do tend to position myself as kind of a lone ranger. I guess I need to change that perception. You know, suck it up and go to more of those meetings I've been avoiding." *(laughs)*

**You:** "It's not just going to the meetings but going in with the attitude that other people are bringing in just as much value as you are. Remember that diversity of thought leads to richer ideas and experiences—which are always good things."

**Foster:** "Right. I hear what you are saying. I need to quit thinking about those meetings as a major time suck and make the effort to get something out of them and really connect with the other people there."

## Step 3: Develop an Action Plan

**You:** "That's a great idea. I'd like to explore ways that I can support you in making that change. I actually have a podcast I would recommend that you check out. I'll send you the link. I also wondered how you might feel about participating in the rotation group that starts in January. That might be a great way to help you learn more about all the other departments in the company, and it would give you plenty of opportunities for collaboration."

**Foster:** "Sounds interesting. I'd like to know more."

**You:** "Great. Let's plan to meet again on the 27th. In the meantime, what action items are you taking away from this?"

**Foster:** "Let's see . . . I will take a look at the podcast you suggested, and I would love to get more information about the rotation program. I think I need to schedule a meeting with the people who report to me and have a hard reset. I know I can do better on that. And if I get invited to some meetings this week, I'll actually go. And I'll listen—really listen—and ask questions. Well, I'll try!" *(laughs)*

## Step 4: Provide Support

**You:** "We are all a work in progress! I'll reach out to human resources and ask them to send you a packet about the rotation program. And if you are headed to a meeting and have some concerns about how to be more collaborative, just stop by. We'll make a game plan."

**Foster:** "Thank you. I appreciate your honesty. I guess I can see how some people might have gotten the impression that I don't care about them or their ideas. That's not the case at all. I just get sort of consumed with deadlines and deliverables. It's a bad habit I need to break. Starting now."

## Step 5: Follow Up

After the meeting, you send Foster the podcast link and email your contact in human resources to share information with Foster about the rotation program. You also schedule another meeting with Foster for the 27th. Finally, with Foster's permission, you reach out to the project manager who is running the meeting on Friday and ask to get feedback afterward about Foster's participation.

• • •

Through this coaching discussion, Foster began to increase his self-awareness and understand how his actions and attitudes were impacting his professional reputation. With you as his coach, Foster started to shift his interactions with others from being efficient transactions to relationship-building communications. Those adjustments will ultimately help Foster make a greater contribution to the team and establish himself as both a technology expert and strong leader.

These outcomes were possible because you came from a place of curiosity, allowing Foster to give you his take on why he thinks and often acts independently. You also did not judge Foster when he responded authentically in terms of how he saw his role as a leader of technology. Instead, you used this as an opportunity to illustrate the implications of his viewpoint. You also helped him to broaden his perspective and see the value of being a leader of people and ideas, not just technology.

Over time, Foster will benefit from the fact that someone interrupted his typical patterns and belief systems, and he will likely expand his impact as a leader and as a colleague. Plus, his opportunities to do more, learn more, and lead more may also increase.

## COACHING BAILEY: JUGGLING THE DEMANDS OF INCREASED RESPONSIBILITY

Bailey is one of the project managers on your team. She is very sharp and has a track record of doing well in terms of her core responsibilities. However, lately you've been getting some feedback from others that she isn't very responsive with her follow-up. You've heard that she seems somewhat scattered and has allowed a few emails to fall through the cracks. That surprises you, given that she seems to make most of her deadlines and has been successful at seeing projects through to completion.

### Getting Started

Before your session, take 10 minutes to think about how you will handle this discussion to get to the root of what is going on. Write down your answers in the spaces below:

- What question should lead off your discussion?

- How can you explore this issue in a way that gives her the benefit of the doubt, based on her generally good performance?

- What support should you offer?

Your first coaching session might start with you saying something like "Hey, Bailey! Nice to see you. What's the latest on the product launch?" Then, you transition to Step 1.

## Step 1: Assess the Situation

**Bailey:** "Well, it's been really hectic. We're falling behind on a few of our deliverables, but I think we can still meet the main deadline . . . as long as we don't have a crisis."

**You:** "I know there are a lot of moving pieces on this one. More departments involved. Probably your biggest project yet. But I'm getting some feedback from team members who are concerned about getting their piece of this launch done. There's some frustration out there. Do you have any idea what's going on ?"

**Bailey:** "I guess there's kind of a disconnect. I'm collaborating with some people I've never worked with before. And let's just say, they have . . . well, different expectations when it comes to response time. Several of them are getting, you know, a little snippy. I mean, I get it. I am kinda buried in email at the moment."

**You:** "Have you talked with any of them about that?"

**Bailey:** "Ummm . . . no. Didn't really want to stir up any extra drama. Just seems sort of unrealistic. They know how many things I'm juggling."

**You:** "Maybe they don't understand. That's a conversation you might consider having. Who knows, part of it may be a perception problem. Even if you get them an answer or whatever they need by the deadline—but it comes in at the *very* last minute—there's a good chance they still might feel like you aren't very responsive or reliable. I know that's not the image you want to project. So why do you think your emails are piling up on you?"

**Bailey:** "I'm not sure there's any one particular reason. I glance through and find the ones that are most important. After I respond to those, I circle back to the others. It just takes some time. Like I said, some people aren't very patient."

## Step 2: Generate Ideas

**You:** "You've always done a good job of following up, but your workload is much heavier now. Maybe we can brainstorm for a minute on ways to help you tackle the email issue. Walk me through how you organize your in-box. What's your system?"

**Bailey:** "My system? *(laughs)* I guess I don't really have one. The emails sit in my in-box until I can get to them. And eventually, I do."

**You:** "Got it. But since this has started having an impact on the team, let's talk about some solutions. What things could you do, starting right now, to get organized and be more responsive in that area?"

**Bailey:** "Well, that's a good question. *(pauses)* I guess my first move would be to block out some time on my calendar every day to get through my email. No interruptions. No excuses. I just need to make that a priority. Ughhh—and turn off my phone!"

**You**: "That sounds reasonable. What else?"

**Bailey:** "Huh . . . let me think. Maybe I could change the way I handle the team meetings. I usually just jump in with the updates and assignments. I guess I could pause first to see if anything needs my attention or ask whether something got overlooked since we last met."

"I could also be more specific about setting expectations for response times. Instead of saying, 'I'll get back to you,' I could say, 'I'll let you know by Friday.' Then they can't be irritated with me starting on Wednesday!" *(laughs)*

**You:** "Good point! Here's another idea. There's a woman named Cara Morris in the research and development division. She's been a project manager for years, and I am always so impressed with the way she keeps everything organized. Files, status updates, emails, all of it. Have you ever met her?"

**Bailey:** "I don't think so."

**You:** "Well, if you'd like, I could introduce you. Maybe she'd be willing to spend a little time with you and show you her system. Not that you would need to copy it, but there might be a few elements there that you could borrow or adapt to your own style."

**Bailey:** "Bring it on! If there's a better way, I'm up for it."

## Step 3: Develop an Action Plan

**You:** "Great! I'll reach out to her as soon as we wrap up here. So, give me a recap. What are the next steps?"

**Bailey:** "I'm going to add dedicated 'email time' to my calendar as a recurring event. Starting today. I'll change the agenda for the next meeting to set aside time up front for tying up any loose threads before we dive in. And then I'll follow up with Cara to see if we can get together later this week."

## Step 4: Provide Support

**You:** "Excellent. Stop by and see me if you want to talk about your strategy for reorganizing once you visit with Cara. Otherwise, let's get together again the week of the 14th after your next team meeting so you can give me an update. And I'll touch base with a few team members in a couple weeks to see if they are feeling better about how the project is moving along. Hopefully, they will notice a difference."

## Step 5: Follow Up

After your meeting, you send an email to Cara and set up another meeting with Bailey the week of the 14th. You also make a note in your calendar to follow up with other team members in two weeks to assess the progress.

• • •

This coaching conversation uncovered an important piece of information. As Bailey began taking on more work, it became obvious that she wasn't as organized as she needed to be. When her team members expressed their frustration, she assumed they were being overly demanding and had unrealistic expectations. However, through conversations with you, Bailey realized that her preferred work process and communication cadence were having a negative impact on some team members. Thankfully, she was open to exploring alternatives and making changes that would result in better relationships with her colleagues and an increase in overall productivity.

What role did you play in helping Bailey recover and maintain her stellar reputation as an excellent project manager? For starters, you didn't automatically assume that she was falling behind or taking less interest in her work. You looked to Bailey's past performance to inform your assessment and, frankly, gave her the benefit of the doubt.

That approach allowed you to accomplish two objectives. First, you helped Bailey to see that larger-scale project work requires enhanced and more specific communication with deliberate touchpoints.

You also helped her realize that her current organizational methods weren't sufficient to handle more complex projects with a broader range of stakeholders—many of whom are new. Once Bailey refined her productivity practices and became more intentional about ensuring that her project team members were getting what they needed, she was better positioned to tackle more projects and maintain her reputation as a solid and effective project manager.

## COACHING HECTOR: CONTRIBUTING IN AN AUTHENTIC WAY

Hector has been on your team for about four months. While Hector gets his work done and meets his deadlines, he seems to be flying under the radar. He is very quiet during team meetings and in his one-on-one meetings with you.

During his interview for the sales enablement job, he impressed you with his knowledge and his responses about taking initiative on team projects. Unfortunately, you haven't seen this in his current role just yet. His job performance could probably be considered satisfactory, but the position really requires someone who is engaged and creative, and who contributes. Hector simply seems disengaged.

### Getting Started

You set up an appointment to meet with Hector for tomorrow morning. Take a moment before reading on to think about the strategy you will use to create the best possible outcome for Hector. Write down your answers in the spaces below:

- How should you set the tone for your initial meeting?


- What questions could you ask to find out Hector's perspective on his position and his projects?


- What outcomes would you like to see as a result of this meeting?


Your coaching session might unfold like this:

**You:** "Good morning, Hector! Come on in. Thanks for agreeing to spend some time with me."

**Hector:** "Ummm, sure. Was I supposed to prepare something for this? I guess I don't really know what this is all about."

**You:** "Not at all. I just wanted to find out more about how things are going with you."

**Hector:** "Uh . . . OK . . . ?"

**You:** "Are you feeling welcomed by the team and like you're adjusting to the company and the new role?"

## Step 1: Assess the Situation

**Hector:** "Yeah, I think so. Trying to take it all in, but I'm getting my bearings. Everyone here has been very kind."

**You:** "So tell me . . . now that you've had a chance to observe how we support the sales team, do you have any ideas or suggestions you'd like to share?"

**Hector:** "Hmmm, I guess I have some thoughts about the translation process for our marketing material."

**You:** "OK, tell me more."

**Hector:** "I think it's really important to make sure the translators use the regional dialect of our customers. Not just the generic foreign language. My previous employer learned that the hard way, and it caused all kinds of problems for us. So many misunderstandings. Probably lost sales."

**You:** "Excellent feedback. And very relevant. I think you probably have a lot of valuable experiences to draw from. Is there anything keeping you from sharing your thoughts with the team or with our internal customers? I've noticed that you seem a little hesitant to speak up during the meetings."

**Hector:** "I . . . I don't know. Uncomfortable, I guess. I don't feel as confident about knowing the products like I did at my last company."

**You:** "That's certainly something we can work on. What would help you feel more comfortable with your grasp of the product specs and applications?"

## Step 2: Generate Ideas

**Hector:** "Well, it would be nice if I could sit down with someone in the product group and ask some questions about their process. That might give me more context. I always feel more knowledgeable when I understand things from that angle."

**You:** "I can make that happen. I'll send an email to one of their managers. Her name is Jean. Super funny and she knows her stuff. We'll set up a time for the two of you to get together. Other than that, is there anything else that might be holding you back from being more proactive as part of the team?"

**Hector:** "Ummm . . . well . . . to be honest, I'm a 'processor.' I may not always have an idea or a suggestion right in the moment. I like to mull things over and let them all marinate before I give feedback. I realize that's not how everybody else around here works, so I guess I've just kinda kept to myself rather than reaching out after the fact."

**You:** "Oh, I totally get that. But please know that we welcome your thoughts before, during, or after the meetings—whenever you have them. We hired you because of your international experience, and we could really use your insights when it comes to supporting the sales team during the global product launch."

**Hector:** "Thanks! I really appreciate that."

**You:** "I tell you what . . . I'll make it a point to remind everyone at the end of our team meetings to share any additional ideas and suggestions in a follow-up email. In the meantime, I would strongly urge you to reach out to your teammates whenever you have an idea. And at the end of meetings with internal clients, you might let them know they may be hearing from you again after you've had time to think about the best ways to set them up for success."

**Hector:** "You know, now I realize that would have been the obvious thing to do. I guess I just felt awkward. I'm still getting to know people, and I didn't want to look like I was a half-step behind by tossing out a suggestion the next day."

## Step 3: Develop an Action Plan

**You:** "Don't let that bother you at all. Again, I think you have a lot to offer our team, and I would love to see you participate more in our meetings and to get more engaged. Let's talk again in two weeks. In the meantime, what are your next steps?"

**Hector:** "I will set up an appointment to meet with Jean in the product group. And, I'll make a conscious effort to circle back to people with my ideas rather than just assuming it's too late."

## Step 4: Provide Support

**You:** "Fantastic. I will touch base with Jean right now. And if you want to run any of your ideas by me regarding the latest product launch, I'm happy to set up another meeting."

## Step 5: Follow Up

After the meeting, you send an email to Jean. You also write yourself a reminder to pay close attention to Hector's level of participation and engagement in meetings. Then, you set up another appointment with Hector in two weeks.

• • •

This coaching session laid the groundwork for helping Hector understand that his insights and expertise are essential for his position on the sales enablement team. Without the benefit of a coaching conversation, a leader might simply have assumed that Hector was bored or lazy. Instead, you identified some key areas for training that would elevate Hector's product knowledge. In addition, you discovered what was contributing to Hector's perceived lack of engagement. Through the process of coaching, Hector will have an opportunity to contribute at a higher level, increase his engagement, and build stronger relationships with his team members and internal customers.

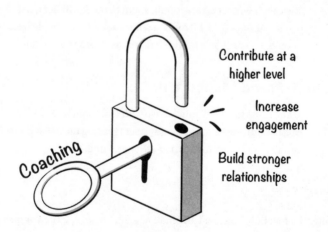

Because Hector gave you the impression during his hiring interview that he would be highly engaged and quick to contribute his expertise to the team, you could have been very frustrated with the reality of the situation. If you just assumed that he was not living up to the initial expectations, you might have encouraged him to move to another position. As a result, the team and the company would have missed out on his valuable insights and experiences. Instead, you approached Hector with a genuine interest in trying to understand what seemed to be holding him back.

You learned several valuable things about him in that conversation. First, Hector does have important input, but he needs time to process it before discussing it. And second, he is much more comfortable contributing when he is intimately familiar with the product or processes involved. Knowing those two things made it easier for you (and others) to tap into his expertise in the future. And, ultimately, you were able to provide him with some solid strategies for capturing the information and the time he needed to feel more confident about sharing his input with the team.

* * *

Performance Coaching can often produce the most direct results among your employees, giving you the tools to help them identify problems and apply solutions. The key to success in this process is to engage in a conversation rather than making it a one-way presentation.

When you approach coaching challenges as a partnership—*with* curiosity and *without* judgment—you dramatically increase the odds of having authentic and meaningful dialogue that allows you to uncover the information you need to coach effectively. That rich data may allow you to point out faulty belief systems or areas of untapped potential that are responsible for the performance gap. By investing the time to help your coachees close that gap, you can be the catalyst that fuels their efforts to make substantive changes with greater impact.

## ESSENTIAL TAKEAWAYS

- The more you practice how you might handle a particular coaching conversation, the easier it will be to translate your thinking strategy into action.

- Performance Coaching is most successful when you engage in a conversation rather than a one-way presentation.

- When you approach coaching challenges as a partnership—with curiosity and without judgment—you dramatically increase the odds of having authentic and meaningful dialogue that allows you to uncover the information you need to coach effectively.

**CHAPTER**

# 7

# Developmental Coaching in Action

**Now that you've had** an opportunity to practice your Performance Coaching strategies, it's time to shift to examples of Developmental Coaching.

As a refresher, Developmental Coaching is focused on helping team members prepare to meet their long-term career goals. Coaches spend time getting to know their employees' strengths, challenges, and career aspirations. Then the coaches strategically help them acquire the experiences and skills (tangible and intangible) needed to advance within the organization.

## COACHING JADE: SUPPORTING YOUR EMPLOYEE'S CAREER ASPIRATIONS

You've been coaching Jade, a woman on your team, who has expressed interest in advancing within the organization. Over the past six months, you've encouraged her to explore other positions in the organization to identify potential fit and interest. At the start of your next one-on-one meeting, she tells you that a position opened up in digital marketing, and she believes it would be a great fit for her.

## Getting Started

Take a moment before reading on to think through the optimal strategy that you would use during the coaching session to create the best possible outcome for Jade. Jot down your answers in the spaces below:

- What's the first question you should ask her?

- What advice should you provide?

- What support should you offer (tangible and emotional)?

- What topics or actions should you avoid?

There's never a one-size-fits-all formula for coaching conversations, but here's an example of how the interaction might progress.

To start, you might say, "Good morning, Jade! Catch me up. What's on your mind today?"

## Step 1: Assess the Situation

**Jade:** "I'm actually really excited. I just heard through the grapevine that a position is opening up in digital marketing. It would be perfect. At least I think so. I've been on the lookout since you and I started talking about opportunities for me to make a move."

**You:** "That's great. Tell me what you know about the job so far."

**Jade:** "I don't have a lot of details yet. I'm guessing it will involve coordinating with the folks in marketing and corporate communications. Maybe the ad agency, too? I'm a little fuzzy on the specifics at this point. I'm kind of nervous and excited at the same time, honestly."

## Step 2: Generate Ideas

**You:** "Based on what you know so far, how do you think your current skills and expertise will fit?"

**Jade:** "Well, you know how much I love everything related to technology. That part would be a no-brainer. And last year I worked quite a bit with the people in marketing when I was assigned to the special project team. They're a hoot. I love them. The way they work is just so different than what I'm doing now. It just . . . it clicked, you know?"

**You:** "Sounds good so far. The technology, the people—clearly—and the way they work all seems to fit, huh? Did you get any exposure to digital marketing when you participated in planning the User Conference? When was that . . . 2020?"

**Jade:** "Oh yeah, I had completely forgotten about that. We had to supply them with some customer analytics."

**You:** "Perhaps you've already done this, but how about talking with some other people who currently hold that position?"

**Jade:** "Hey, that's a good idea. I think there's a guy I met during the User Conference who's still on the team. Maybe I could ask him some questions."

**You:** "That's a good start. Talking to him should be helpful. One, it will give you some more insight into what the expectations are for the role and help you figure out if that's really something you'd want to do on a full-time basis. And second, going into the interview with a leg up on what their current challenges are could give you a nice advantage, right?"

**Jade:** "For sure. I know of at least four other people who are interested in applying for the job, so I want to make sure I stand out."

**You:** "Wow, I guess digital marketing is attracting a lot of folks. Let's think about ways to have you stand out. Would you like me to introduce you to someone else I know in that area?"

**Jade:** "Could you? I would love that."

**You:** "Happy to do it. Let's talk a little about how you might approach these informal meetings to gather more information.

What kinds of questions could you ask to get the most valuable feedback?"

**Jade:** "What do you mean? Like email them questions in advance?"

**You:** "That's one option. Or you could talk to them in person or on Zoom. That might give you the chance to ask some follow-up questions if they say something that's intriguing . . . or confusing . . . or doesn't really tell you what you want to know."

**Jade:** "Good point. I guess I would ask about what the typical day looks like. Maybe ask what kinds of things they're responsible for. Does that sound too lame? If it's not too awkward, I would also want to know what they love most about the position and what they hate."

**You:** "Those are great questions. You might also ask them to describe the biggest challenges their teams are facing right now. That might be beneficial in the interview process. You can use that information to explain specifically how your skills can be used to help offset their biggest pain points."

**Jade:** "That makes sense. I can do that."

## Step 3: Develop an Action Plan

**You:** "So, have you actually applied for the job yet? Or what are your next steps?"

**Jade:** "I wanted to talk with you first, but I'll get on it this afternoon. I need to make a list of questions and set up appointments to meet with both of our contacts in the department. And then I need to prepare for the interview. You know I need my prep time!"

## Step 4: Provide Support

**You:** "That sounds like a great plan! If you'd like me to look through your questions or your notes, just let me know. I might be able to provide some additional guidance there. In the meantime, I'll send you the contact information for the woman I know over there. Sound good? Still nervous?"

**Jade:** "Actually no. Thank you so much!"

## Step 5: Follow Up

After the meeting, you make a note in your calendar to follow up with Jade in one week to see how the process is going and offer any additional assistance, if needed.

• • •

This coaching discussion helped Jade to begin thinking more strategically about the process of applying for the new position. By collecting more information about the requirements and then connecting the dots to her own skills and talents, she can essentially vet herself in a way that is more meaningful for the hiring manager. This kind of preparation gives Jade the best possible opportunity to be considered as a top candidate for the job.

Approaching this coaching session as an opportunity to support your employee's interests speaks volumes about your commitment to growing others. Because you offered to connect Jade with the right people and take steps to increase her visibility with key decision makers, her loyalty to you and the company increased. Her job satisfaction got a major bump. Whether Jade remains in her current role or eventually moves on, the genuine effort you made to help her learn more about the digital marketing job and position herself as a viable candidate showcases your value as a coach and a leader.

Connecting your coachee to the right
people leads to increased loyality

## COACHING ERIK: SUPPORTING YOUR EMPLOYEE'S PROGRESSIVE SUCCESS

Erik is a 35-year-old cybersecurity engineer who has been with the company for eight years and just transferred to your department. He has solid experience and is known for innovative thinking. His previous manager shared with you that Erik is interested in leading more projects and potentially moving into management. From everything you've seen so far, he seems to be an excellent addition to your team.

Last week, you ran into one of the project managers and asked how things were going, particularly with the recent addition of Erik. She said there was no doubt about his intelligence, product knowledge, and commitment to the team, but his presentation skills were falling short. His explanations were overly technical, his points were long-winded, and he simply wasn't engaging his audience.

Knowing that Erik wants to advance within the company, you make a mental note to bring up this topic at the end of your next one-on-one meeting. That's the time you typically dedicate to discussing your employees' developmental career goals and providing support.

## Getting Started

Before reading on, give some thought to how you will structure your conversation to get the best possible outcome for Erik. Jot down your answers in the spaces below:

- How should you bring up this subject to encourage improvement rather than dampen Erik's spirit?


- What specific skills does Erik need to be more successful in this area?


- What kind of support could you offer?

Your conversation with Erik might begin like this:

**You:** "OK, so it sounds like we are on track. Do you have what you need to get started on the network audit?"

**Erik:** "Yes, all set."

**You:** "Super! I also want to just check in and see how you are doing. You had to hit the ground running when you joined the team. We threw a lot at you during the very first week. How do you think it's going so far?"

## Step 1: Assess the Situation

**Erik:** "Pretty well, I would say. We did things a little differently in my previous department, but I'm figuring it out. There's the usual learning curve, of course."

**You:** "It does take some time, but I hear you are jumping right in—which I love! Cassandra called a few days ago and said you've already made some good suggestions for streamlining the risk assessment process. That's fantastic . . . keep those ideas coming!"

**Erik:** "Oh good. I'm glad I've been able to help."

**You:** "You definitely have. I know you're also getting involved with making presentations to some of the internal teams. As I recall, that's not something you did on a regular basis in your last position. How are you feeling about this being a bigger part of your role?"

**Erik:** "Ummm . . . Let's just say the engineering stuff comes easier to me than speaking in front of a group. *(laughs)* I guess

I'll get the hang of it. Sometimes it seems like I'm not getting my points across."

**You:** "In what way? Tell me more about that."

**Erik:** "Well, I typically have about 20 minutes to brief others, and I have to cram a whole lot of information into that time frame. It always seems rushed, and I'm still not covering everything. But the details really matter, you know? That's the point. I want to give them all the critical data."

## Step 2: Generate Ideas

**You:** "Yeah, I talked with the project manager last week. She said it's clear that you know your stuff inside and out, but sometimes people in the audience seem distracted or start checking their phones by the end of your briefings. Do you think you're trying to cover too much in 20 minutes? Could you maybe stick with a high-level focus for the business group and save the nitty-gritty for product development?"

**Erik:** "Well, so far I've been using the same presentation and PowerPoint deck. I suppose I could use some guidance on that."

**You:** "Absolutely. That's an important step in the process. Here's what I've discovered. My presentations are always better when I resist the urge to dive right into building my deck. I have to force myself to stop and think about the audience first. How much do they already know about the topic? Am I starting from scratch or just providing updates? Are these people familiar with the technology I'm discussing? What problem are they trying to solve, and how does my information fit into that? That keeps me focused."

**Erik:** "Oh . . . I'm thinking back about the people I spoke to last week when it didn't seem to go very well. Answering those questions would have made a big difference."

**You:** "The good news is, you'll know for next time! If you can start with those questions, you can build a presentation that's really effective for your audience. You'll have a road map to figure out which facts are relevant and how to share those so people will understand them. Most people don't speak 'engineering' like you do." *(laughs)*

**Erik:** "Makes sense. That's a good strategy."

**You:** "Anything else you'd like to work on?"

**Erik:** "Ehhh . . . sometimes when I get nervous, I feel like I'm just standing there reading my notes out loud. It probably is a little boring, to be fair. I just haven't had a lot of practice with this, but I do want to get better at it."

**You:** "So, you haven't had any formal presentation training in the past?"

**Erik:** "Not really. When the company sponsored the Toastmasters Club about five years ago, I went to a couple of meetings but never really got into it. Maybe I should have stuck it out."

## Step 3: Develop an Action Plan

**You:** "Never too late to learn something new. I know that our leadership and development departments offer a communication and presentation skills course once a quarter. If you are interested, we should get you signed up."

**Erik:** "I'm sure that would be good for me. Probably way out of my comfort zone, but that's why I need it."

**You:** "I actually think you might enjoy it. You'll get a partner during the class that you can meet with over the next three to six months to practice what you learned. I've seen people make huge improvements once they know the strategies and get regular feedback. In the meantime, maybe I can help you streamline one of your project briefings so you can try some new approaches right away. Let's plan to meet on Friday so I can see your deck and offer some suggestions."

**Erik:** "That would be great. I'm anxious to get started, and I would love to take that course."

## Step 4: Provide Support

**You:** "Fantastic! I will send you the link to the registration page so you can sign up."

**Erik:** "Thanks!"

## Step 5: Follow Up

After your coaching session, you send the registration link to Erik and schedule another meeting with him on Friday.

• • •

Through this coaching session, Erik gained confidence about his contributions to the new team while discovering an area with opportunities for improvement. When he learns to better connect with his audiences—influencing rather than just informing—he will increase the positive outcomes from his presentations. Becoming more targeted and engaging in his role as a speaker will also help Erik grow and take charge of his career trajectory.

With everything else on your plate, you could have brushed past the project manager's comment about Erik and his less-than-stellar presentation skills. Instead, you made a mental note to investigate the problem because Erik is a valuable and loyal employee who has his heart set on working at the next level. You know it is your job as a leader to help him accomplish that goal, and exceptional public speaking skills will be a pivotal part of that equation.

Rather than just recommending that Erik sign up for a class, you approached the coaching challenge from a broader and deeper perspective. You spent time getting a real sense of Erik's experience with group presentations and understanding how he typically prepares for briefings. What you uncovered helped to shape your feedback and development suggestions.

Knowing that Erik wants to influence others and distinguish himself as more than just a subject matter expert, you guided him to think in terms of "communicating to engage and influence" rather than just "communicating to inform." Pairing that advice with helpful strategies for presentation development and the offer to help before the next briefing gave Erik a well-rounded approach to elevating his abilities.

So many professionals are never given the opportunity to sharpen their presentation skills. But you recognized this was an important component in Erik's development, and you didn't hesitate to support him in advancing those skills.

## COACHING AMANDA: MOVING FROM DOER TO DRIVER

Amanda has been on your team for more than three years, and she is a standout employee. She's developed a reputation for being extremely organized, reliable, hardworking, and friendly. However, you sense that she is frustrated because yet another one of her peers—someone who has been in the same position as Amanda, but for less time—was recently tapped for a promotion. Amanda has asked to meet with you tomorrow to talk about the situation and her future with the company.

### Getting Started

Pause for a moment to think about the strategy you will use in your conversation with Amanda. Jot down your answers in the spaces provided:

- How can you empathize with her frustration while prompting her to uncover the developmental needs she may have been overlooking?



- What support could you provide to help Amanda grow and position herself as a stronger candidate for promotion?

- What do you think will be the biggest roadblock during your conversation?

Your meeting might go something like this:

**You:** "Good morning, Amanda. Please tell me what's on your mind today."

**Amanda:** "I wanted to talk to you about the supervisor role that was recently filled."

**You:** "Sure. Tell me what you're feeling."

## Step 1: Assess the Situation

**Amanda:** "I'm not going to lie, I really thought I had a shot at that one. Not that Julia won't do a great job, but I feel like I've stepped up my game lately. I've picked up more of the status reporting duties. Covered for so many people when they were out. Worked overtime to meet all the crazy deadlines at the end of the year. And every time I produce a customer profile for sales, I get rave reviews. I even got that award last spring. I don't know what else I could have possibly done to be seen as the front-runner for that position. I just don't get it."

**You:** "Well, first of all, please know that you are a very valuable member of this team. You work hard and do a fantastic job. With that said, those aren't the only factors considered when choosing someone for a management position."

**Amanda:** "OK, so should I work on getting another certification or consider going back to school to get my MBA to balance out my domain expertise?"

## Step 2: Generate Ideas

**You:** "Let's hold those thoughts for a minute. What do you think qualifies someone to be a good leader? Try not to refer to their credentials or expertise. Just describe their intangible skills and attributes you associate with leaders."

**Amanda:** "Ummm . . . dedicated to the company . . . good with people . . . organized and efficient."

**You:** "Yes. But what about someone who knows how to paint a vivid picture of what success looks like for their team members? Think about the person who can demonstrate the link between the team's daily activities and the organization's success. Great leaders don't just try to meet their own objectives. They use their experiences and curiosity to make decisions that better position the company for the future. Those aren't things you can achieve by finishing your to-do list. They're more strategic. It's less about being a doer and more about being a driver."

**Amanda:** "Huhh . . . I never really thought of it that way. I'm definitely a doer. And I suppose that's working against me. It's unfortunate because I've always followed the principle that you can get ahead if you're productive and organized and work really hard. I guess there's more to it than that."

**You:** "There definitely is. So, if your goal is to be seen as someone ready to move up in the organization, what kinds of things could you do to create that perception? To show that you can be a driver and not just a doer?"

**Amanda:** "Well, let me think about that . . . I probably need to delegate more. Which is a challenge for me. Whatever it is, I can usually do it faster than I can explain to somebody else how to do it, you know? Maybe stop volunteering to take notes at every single meeting, even though mine would be more thorough." *(laughs)*

**You:** "Those make a great start. Another option is to deliberately change the way you think about all of your projects. Don't get bogged down in the details. Remind yourself that your value isn't tied to what you produce or how many things you check off your list. Shift to the big picture. Think long term. Strategic. And then make it a point to speak up and share your insights from those perspectives. That demonstrates that you are thinking like a leader."

**Amanda:** "I can do that. I mean, I'm sure it's harder than it sounds, but that's good advice."

**You:** "It would also help if people could start envisioning you in a leadership role. Think about that in terms of the way you show up every day, literally and figuratively. Not just what you wear, although that can be part of it. Your energy level. Your enthusiasm for the problems we aim to solve. In other words, do you look, sound, and act like a leader? Or someone who is an individual contributor? The two make very different impressions."

**Amanda:** "Oooh, I know what you mean by that. Some people just have that leader vibe. Kind of hard to describe, but you know it when you see it."

**You:** "Exactly. And you can begin to adopt those qualities. You know, we have a special project coming up in April. Maybe you could volunteer to lead the committee organizing that. Might give you an opportunity to showcase your skills and show everyone how well you can function in that role."

**Amanda:** "I would love that! It sounds perfect."

**You:** "OK, let's plan to get together again in two weeks. In the meantime, what will you be working on to help you meet your goal?"

## Step 3: Develop an Action Plan

**Amanda:** "I know it's early, but I would like to volunteer right this moment to lead the project in April. Sign me up! I also bought a book about a year ago on strategic thinking, and it's been collecting dust on my bookshelf. I will be reading that, starting tonight. And I'm going to spend some more time thinking about what I might be doing or saying that gives the impression I'm not ready to advance. I think you really hit on something there. Not sure why that didn't occur to me before, but I appreciate your taking the time to talk with me about all of this."

## Step 4: Provide Support

**You:** "Absolutely. I'll get back to you with more details on the special project. And if you have some other ideas about how to demonstrate your leadership potential, let's talk about them."

## Step 5: Follow Up

Right as the meeting ends, you jot down a reminder that Amanda will be leading the project in April. You also schedule a follow-up meeting with her. After that, you make a mental note to pay attention to how she contributes in meetings and whether or not she starts spending more time looking at things from the treetops versus the weeds going forward.

● ● ●

This coaching conversation could create a significant change in Amanda's career trajectory. She simply didn't realize that *doing more* wasn't the key to being considered for advancement. You were able to help her identify some simple ways to begin changing the perception and reality of her as a doer rather than a driver. With some time and a shift in focus, she will be better positioned as a viable candidate for the next management opening.

It's hard to get an achievement-oriented "doer" to believe that nontechnical and intangible skills are just as important for advancement as technical know-how, business acumen, and results. But that's exactly what you did here. Not by shaming her or shoving it in her face, but by getting Amanda to reflect on what really makes a great leader.

Is leadership defined by delivering exceptional pivot tables and airtight budgets? No! It's more about the ability to handle short-term challenges while also thinking about long-term implications. It's about managing work *and* inspiring action. Holding people accountable for their performance while helping them reach their highest potential.

Had you not invested in this coaching conversation with Amanda, she might have let her frustration with this experience erode her trust in the organization. But instead of taking her aspirations for a leadership role to another company, she is now learning how to apply her skills in a different way. Thanks to you, Amanda feels valued and is excited about possibilities for advancement on your team (or beyond) using her new approach as a "driver."

. . . .

Strong Developmental Coaching can become a leader's signature contribution to an organization's success. Guiding young professionals in their growth—helping them to acquire new skills, refine their intangible characteristics, and learn the nuances of applying those attributes—is one of the most important ways to ensure that a company will survive and thrive in the years ahead.

Requiring equal parts of curiosity and patience, Developmental Coaching is a worthy investment in your team's human capital. When it's done well, it can be a game changer for employees, leaders, and the companies they support.

## ESSENTIAL TAKEAWAYS

- Developmental Coaching is focused on helping team members prepare to meet their long-term career goals.

- Connecting your coachees to the right people not only helps increase their visibility, but also strengthens loyalty to you and the company.

- Guiding young professionals in their growth through coaching is one of the most important ways to ensure a company will survive and thrive in the years ahead.

CHAPTER

8

# Common Obstacles
# for Coaches

**Organizations that deliberately support** a coaching climate can reap huge benefits. The same goes for the managers who support coaching, as well as the team members who participate.

With that said, being a leader-coach comes with challenges. Knowing what to expect and being prepared with some smart coping strategies can help you overcome these common obstacles.

Let's dive into 10 of these obstacles together.

## NOT ENOUGH TRAINING OR CONFIDENCE

The truth is business coaching is very different than the sports coaching examples we've experienced in real life or seen on TV. Real-life coaching requires training and confidence. Without these tools, coaching is near impossible.

For example, your boss may have coached a T-ball team five years ago and now thinks, *I know how to motivate people—even four-year-olds! I'll be a great coach!* People like this dive into coaching in the workplace without the proper training and context to understand the real purpose of coaching. They confuse it with mentoring, training, or counseling. They also lack any specific plans beyond taking on the role of enthusiastic cheerleader. And—no surprise here—they don't get the results they should.

On the other hand, I've watched hundreds of leaders shy away from taking a more active approach to coaching because they were intimidated by the process or felt ill-equipped to do it effectively. Again, the potential for great outcomes isn't there.

So, what's the solution?

Well, I'll boost your confidence right away because you're already ahead of the game by reading this book and making the commitment to learn the skills needed for effective coaching. Adopting a positive mindset and following a proven coaching model will only increase your impact. Practice regularly the coaching methods we've already talked about, and don't be afraid to ask for honest feedback from those you coach. That input can be incredibly valuable as you refine your coaching techniques.

It's also helpful to remember that fantastic coaches don't have to be perfect and they don't have to know everything. They just need a willingness to listen, ask smart questions, and be supportive. Once you are armed with the proper training and a big dose of confidence, you'll be well on your way to coaching success.

## NOT ENOUGH TIME

Generally speaking, leaders have a whole lot on their plates. Attending countless meetings. Managing others. Trying to get their own work done. They are constantly under pressure to do more—and do it faster. The idea of adding something like coaching to the long, long list of daily requirements may seem overwhelming.

This perception of "not enough time" is one of the biggest obstacles for coaches.

While there is no way to add hours to your day, I can encourage you to shuffle your priorities and remember the extraordinary benefits coaching can deliver. Think of it this way: above all else, your job as a leader is to build a high-performing team that can meet or exceed goals. While it may seem counterintuitive at first to focus more intensely on your team members than your deliverables and deadlines, that strategy actually maximizes your results. Once you make coaching a top priority, you'll begin to understand how the paradox is actually a secret to success.

Investing your time and energy to elevate the quality of performance among your team members *will* pay off. Employees who sense your commitment to their growth will support you, as well as the goals you are trying to accomplish as a team.

That's compelling stuff, but I can guess what you're thinking: *As great as that sounds, my calendar is jam-packed. There's no way to squeeze in anything else.*

I hear you! But stay with me for a moment and think through your options. What tasks can you off-load or delegate to find a few hours a week for formal coaching sessions? Is there something you always do or a meeting you regularly attend that's become more of a habit rather than a productive action? What would happen if you stopped doing that? Would it really matter? You might be surprised at the number of things you can remove from your schedule if you get serious about determining what really adds value (and what doesn't).

With a little creativity, you can also shoehorn some informal coaching into the small spaces in your day. Maybe you plan 15-minute check-in calls with your team members during your daily commute. Or you have quarterly lunch plans with each person for an extended one-on-one session. Find a solution that works for you as well as those you lead.

Consider also real-time coaching. Never underestimate the value of five uninterrupted minutes to offer some immediate feedback, give praise, provide encouragement, or share some gentle constructive criticism on the spot. These small moments of coaching can add up and lead to real progress.

Great! So, the time issue is resolved now, right? Well, no, not exactly.

Trust me when I tell you, those hours you've carefully set aside for coaching need to be protected. Suddenly there's a fire to put out. The client moves up the deadline. The big presentation for tomorrow isn't ready yet. When facing those inevitable schedule crunches, it can be tempting to think a coaching session is the easiest thing to move.

Don't do it.

Coaching needs to be a nonnegotiable part of your routine, despite the circumstances and chaos. Constantly cancelling or rescheduling meetings with team members sends a strong negative message to others about your commitment to their growth. Instead, demonstrate that you are all in to support your team members, even when (actually, especially when!) things are hectic. Showing that level of dedication to the people you coach will lead to amazing results. After all, you're sharing with them one of your most important resources: *your time.*

## NOT ESTABLISHING RAPPORT

*OK, I get it. Coaching is going to transform the productivity of my team. I've set aside some time each week to make it happen. I have suggestions. I have tools. How much coaching can I cram into an hour? Let's get this party started!*

Great thinking . . . . but not so fast.

Effective coaching isn't about burying your employee in "helpful" information as he or she stares back at you with a deer-in-headlights look. Coaching involves trust, honest dialogue, and an *actual* relationship. It takes time to build those things and create an authentic emotional connection. Neglecting that is like driving down a dead-end street.

So be deliberate about really getting to know the people you coach. Are you familiar with their backgrounds, families, and personal goals? All of those factor into the career goals they have in mind. The only way to be successful in supporting people along their career journeys is to understand their backstories.

The concept of building rapport hints at two-way communication. Yes, respect your position as a leader, but don't be afraid to share some of your career struggles. Displaying that vulnerability can strengthen the bond between coach and coachee, allowing for deeper conversations and more meaningful outcomes.

Even if you're anxious to accelerate the coaching process on the way to big results, you simply can't skip this step. Invest the time to develop a sense of trust and rapport. When you do, the coaching you provide will be remarkably more powerful.

## NOT BEING FULLY PRESENT

Leaders have to wear many hats: strategist, manager, visionary, problem solver, motivator—and the list goes on. Understandably, your attention gets pulled in many directions during the course of a day (or even an hour).

But for coaching to be effective, the employee sitting in front of you needs to feel like you are fully focused on them, genuinely interested in their progress, and invested in their career.

To create that perception of absolute focus requires discipline on your part. That means temporarily blocking out all the emails, text messages, phone calls, and papers on your desk so you can give your team member your complete attention. Here's the hitch. Even when you find a way to ignore all the outside communications, you also have to manage the thoughts and emotions that are competing for your mental bandwidth.

Thoughts like: *What time do I need to leave here so I can pick up my dry cleaning before they close? I could really go for a bag of M&Ms right now. Did I add sandwich bags to the grocery list? I can't forget to book the hotel for Benita's wedding next month.*

Suffice it to say, there will be plenty of forces—internal and external—trying to sabotage your focus during coaching sessions. It's not easy to fight them all off, but with solid intentions and some practice, you can learn to be present and fully engaged for relatively short spans of time.

Commit to the process and prove to your team members that you are truly in it for them.

## NOT CONNECTING THE DOTS BETWEEN DAILY PERFORMANCE AND BROADER GOALS

Many leaders approach the coaching process with a laser-tight focus: helping their direct reports achieve maximum performance. That's the whole point, right?

Well . . . kind of. That's part of it, but not the *whole* point.

One common obstacle that trips up many coaches is forgetting to help their coachees make a connection between their day-to-day efforts and their career aspirations, as well as the larger goal of contributing to the organization's success. Providing that big-picture context to their career and the company is critical in helping employees connect with the larger purpose of their work. It's also important to establish that mindset as you develop the future leaders for the company.

> "I can really tell a difference in the quality of your work since you took that development course on strategic planning. Your last presentation was right on target. In fact, the executive team will be using some of your ideas as part of the corporate objective to improve the customer experience. Nice work! In fact, I think you're ready to represent the team at the company's next all-hands meeting."

It's admirable as a coach to do everything in your power to help your team members perform at their highest levels. Just remember to connect their individual results and success on a larger scale: accelerating their own career journeys while generating positive outcomes for the company.

## NOT VALUING THE IMPORTANCE OF DIFFERENT COMMUNICATION STYLES

In many ways, leaders have to be chameleons. Their best chance of generating great results is to truly understand the people on their teams: what motivates them, what crushes them, what makes them tick, and what ticks them off. Each person is different, so if you manage each person as though they are the same, both you and your coachees will probably fall short of your goals.

The same principle applies to communication during the coaching process. The pumped-up, high-energy coaching conversations you have with the very extroverted Christy probably won't work well with the quiet, introverted Shawn.

Take time to consider how your communication style affects the people you coach, and think about the subtle shifts you can make individually to increase your impact. I'm not in any way suggesting that you adopt a wildly different persona depending on who's sitting in your office, but you *can* improve your coaching outcomes by taking a more nuanced approach to your communications and adapting in real time for different settings and situations.

If Christy just lost her biggest account, the coaching conversation that day calls for more empathy than energy, such as:

> "Rough day, huh? I'm sorry to hear things didn't end up the way we hoped."

> "I know how hard you worked to keep that client happy."

> "How are you feeling about the whole thing?"

Even though Christy is normally a go-getter of epic proportions, her coach knew it wasn't the right time to discuss all the things that contributed to the lost account and generate ideas for preventing that in the future.

Great coaches really know the individuals they're coaching, and they constantly "read the room." They closely observe the impact they are having on others and adjust as needed. Sometimes that means graciously defusing a heated discussion, picking up on the need to clarify a certain point, explaining a concept in more basic terms, or realizing the best tactic at that moment is to hold back an idea rather than push it forward.

# NOT PURSUING OTHERS' PERSPECTIVES

In today's world, teams will inevitably include people of different ages, genders, cultures, social and ethnic backgrounds, religions, and sexual orientations. Organizations that recognize the value in diversity can tap into a powerful synergy of thought that fuels greater innovation. But what happens if individual leaders don't recognize this value in their coaching relationships and conversations? What if they don't actively pursue diversity of thought? There's likely a range of outcomes, and none of them are positive.

As human beings with unique backgrounds and experiences, we see the world through our own lenses. We have a distinct point of view that colors the way we interpret everything around us. And, because of that point of view, we tend to believe that our view is the right one. It makes perfect sense to us. Here are some examples:

> "There's only one viable solution to this problem, and that's selling the subsidiary."

> "Obviously we need to hold the event in California. That's where 82 percent of our clients are located."

> "We can't wait until fourth quarter to upgrade our systems. That has to happen now."

Sometimes it seems almost shocking when others don't see things the same way we do. Even if we try to be intentional about having an open mind, we don't always succeed at welcoming other points of view. This can be a big problem when it comes to coaching.

To move past this obstacle, push yourself to be the kind of coach who not only invites divergent thinking but deliberately seeks it out. Prompt the people you are leading to push the boundaries. Help them feel comfortable tossing out ideas that aren't just the same old, same old. Their distinct perspectives are valuable and can shine light on new opportunities. "What alternatives have we missed? Is there a reason our usual approach might not work anymore? Is there a better way?" "You know my opinion, but can you prove me wrong?"

If you are attempting to guide a team member to generate ideas during a coaching session, you lose credibility if you discount all suggestions and strategies, including those that don't fit into your particular view of the problem. Pause to think and suspend judgment. Is that idea the dumbest thing you've ever heard or, is it just crazy enough to be brilliant? Challenge yourself and remain open to the possibility that it's the latter.

As a coach, remember that humility is an essential ingredient, too. Never assume you know it all or that your solutions are the only valid options. Shift your mindset and adopt the approach that you can learn something new from every single person you coach. Their thought processes. Their perspectives. Their insights. Many of the most successful, longtime coaches will tell you that they have learned incredible lessons from their coachees through the years—all because they valued diverse thoughts.

Make it a point to show a genuine interest in people with divergent views. Remain open, and welcome new perspectives. The results of your coaching are sure to improve.

## NOT ELIMINATING PERSONAL BIAS

Well, this topic is a little . . . *awkward*.

No matter how personable and friendly you are, you will inevitably end up needing to coach someone you, frankly, don't like very much. Maybe there's a personality conflict. Or you don't agree with this person's past tactics. Or you've heard too many rumors about their questionable choices or behaviors.

Whatever it is, you simply are not on the same wavelength as the person you are coaching. From your first coaching session with this person, the message running through your brain is something like: *Total waste of time. This person is uncoachable . . . at least by me! Doomed to fail.*

As you might guess, that attitude creates a self-fulfilling prophecy in the coaching relationship. It is absolutely doomed to fail.

You must clear your mind of all the preconceived ideas about this person and their potential. Set aside the bias. Shelve any agendas. Commit to reframing the situation and the conversations from a coaching perspective.

Your goal as a leader and coach is to create a high-performing team, and this perhaps-less-than-pleasant part of the process is an important way to achieve the goal. Remind yourself that you will be successful if this person is successful. And, perhaps think about this experience as a challenge. Search for evidence that contradicts the negative impression you have of this person. What positive attributes can you identify? How is the person making progress or adding value? What do you have in common with him or her?

If you can coach objectively and compassionately, you might just discover that the rumor mill got it all wrong.

On the flip side, what happens if your initial suspicions turn out to be correct? Maybe this person is truly uninterested, unmotivated, and uncoachable. You can't control that, but you still take away the valuable experience you gained during the process. You built important coaching skills by working to remain neutral and approaching topics with a sense of curiosity rather than judgment. That effort is never wasted. In fact, it will likely serve you well in the near future.

## NOT ENOUGH PATIENCE

Even the most brilliant coach on the planet can't transform a subpar worker into a high potential employee overnight. There's no magic wand or a quick fix. It takes time, and let's face it, impatience can creep in and zap our enthusiasm for the whole process.

Sometimes you have team members who just haven't warmed up to the coaching relationship yet. Or you may feel like they have a consistent pattern of two steps forward and one step back. That frustration can begin to undermine your coaching efforts. You may find yourself thinking:

> *Doesn't he realize this is a great opportunity to accelerate his career? How can he not see it?*

> *She tells me she wants to be considered for management, but then she doesn't follow through on any of the action plans we talk about.*

> *There's no other explanation. He just doesn't care.*

If coaches allow those attitudes to permeate all their interactions with the team members they coach, the process is going to languish. Impatience can become poison.

So, how can you overcome this obstacle?

Remind yourself that great coaching is a marathon, not a sprint. Try to maintain the hope that some aspect of the process will eventually ignite a fire in your team members and change the pace of their career growth. Let that hope become the fuel that pushes you to get more creative as a coach.

Here's one way to think about it. We can't control the actions (or reactions) of the people we coach. But we *can* control our own attitudes and behaviors. If we're feeling impatient because the process isn't moving as quickly as we'd like, we shouldn't automatically assume the problem lies with our team members. Instead, think about some pointed questions like these:

> *As a coach, am I providing encouragement and motivation in a way that is most meaningful for this team member?*
>
> *Am I offering the right kind of support to help them be successful?*
>
> *What changes or improvements could I make to generate a better coaching outcome?*
>
> *How could I get this person involved with an assignment they'd be really passionate about?*

When you uncover opportunities to actively help the coaching process move forward, you may find that your impatience evaporates and makes way for positive emotions that contribute to a better-performing team.

## NOT BEING IN THE SAME LOCATION AS THE PEOPLE YOU COACH

This is an obstacle that has gained serious attention in recent years when so many people around the globe transitioned to working remotely. Since virtual coaching is now the rule rather than the exception for many companies, the next chapter is devoted solely to this fascinating and timely topic.

## ESSENTIAL TAKEAWAYS

- Fantastic coaches don't have to be perfect or know everything, but they do need a willingness to listen, ask smart questions, and be supportive.

- Your job as a leader is to build a high-performing team that can meet or exceed goals.

- Coaching needs to be a nonnegotiable part of your routine, despite the circumstances and chaos.

- Never assume you know it all or that your solutions are the only valid options; you can learn something new from every person you coach.

CHAPTER

9

# Coaching in a Virtual Environment

**Advances in technology over** the past few decades have enabled more employees to work remotely than ever before. These advances have also allowed organizations to hire top talent from halfway around the globe and offer more flexible working conditions to all employees. This remote-work trend has been on the rise for years, but nothing accelerated it more than the global pandemic that impacted the world beginning in 2020.

Unless people were working in some type of direct service industry, employers and employees had no choice but to (quickly) figure out how to get their jobs done from home. Professionals set up desk spaces and Zoom backgrounds. They stocked up on technology and gadgets that helped them do their work from home and stay connected with their colleagues. The benefits? Not having to commute. Doing their work in casual attire. And taking meetings from the sofa.

Today, most people believe the "new normal" for business will involve some type of hybrid solution for employees—meaning they spend their time working partially remote and partially in person. Organizations will likely have to develop many innovative strategies to accommodate this rapidly evolving business environment and the needs of their workers, but one thing is for sure: coaching will be—and needs to be—part of the mix.

In fact, according to a report published in July 2021, McKinsey & Company surveyed 500 senior executives in a variety of industries to find out how they handled the sudden shift to a remote workforce during the pandemic. The findings were conclusive. Companies that showed improved financial performance during the time of the study also increased their spending on coaching by 49 percent.[*] In other words, they doubled down on coaching even if it had to be virtual. And it paid off.

What does all of this mean for you as a leader-coach? You will almost certainly have to conduct at least some portion of your coaching sessions in a virtual environment, and there's a good chance it might be all of them. In this chapter, I'll share the pros and cons of that reality and provide some guidelines to help maximize the effectiveness of your online coaching sessions.

## ADVANTAGES OF COACHING VIRTUALLY

Coaching may have traditionally been a face-to-face endeavor. But when it's done well, virtual coaching can be just as effective for enabling

---

[*] "Return as a Muscle," *McKinsey Quarterly*, 2021, https://www.mckinsey.com /business-functions/people-and-organizational-performance/our-insights/return -as-a-muscle-how-lessons-from-covid-19-can-shape-a-robust-operating-model -for-hybrid-and-beyond.

your employees to develop their skills, engage with their teams, and improve productivity metrics.

## Flexibility and Convenience

Transportation hassles and long commutes in bad weather are avoided when virtual coaching is an option. There's no need to reserve a conference room or put on formal business attire. All you need is a decent internet connection, and you can coach from pretty much anywhere at any time.

This also means scheduling is less of a hassle and you have versatility in how you structure your coaching sessions. It's hard to beat the convenience of virtual coaching!

## Comfortability, Physically and Emotionally

Coaching virtually eliminates the unspoken power differential that comes with sitting in your office and the too-formal feeling of giant leather chairs in the conference room. In the virtual world, coachees have likely created a space in their homes where they feel confident, safe, and in control. That's particularly important if your coaching conversations involve a difficult topic or one that requires a higher level of confidentiality.

## Focusability

Being able to use a video service like Zoom is a huge benefit for coaching because you can focus on the faces of those you're coaching. All of the extraneous elements that might distract you during an in-person coaching session are essentially cropped out in the virtual format. You don't see an overflowing trash can *(Did the cleaning service not show up last night?)* or a half-eaten bagel on the desk *(I didn't see bagels in the breakroom this morning. Wonder if they have cream cheese . . .).*

Coaching in the virtual environment edits out these types of distractions and the internal dialog that can inadvertently follow and take your mind down the proverbial rabbit hole. Being on video basically forces you to concentrate on the screen view of your coachees from the neck up and allows you to pinpoint all of your attention on their words, facial expressions, and tone of voice. That level of focus can increase your ability to actively listen to the people you coach, get a "read" on how they are responding to your comments, and make adjustments in real time if you sense a disconnect.

## Frequency of Support

The Covid-19 pandemic compelled many leader-coaches to replace their monthly, in-person one-on-one meetings with weekly, virtual check-ins. They understood that their coachees were often experiencing stress and isolation, and the typical pattern of longer, less frequent coaching sessions wasn't serving them well during that time. The well-being of their team members needed to take a front seat, and the virtual environment made that an easy change to implement.

If you sense that your coachees need more frequent contact with you, virtual coaching gives you a fast, easy way to provide that level of support. Brief, face-to-face contact—even without the physical presence of being in the same room—goes a long way toward ensuring your conversations don't get lost in translation and reminds coachees that they are a priority in your schedule.

Another advantage of more frequent coaching connections is building greater accountability into the process. Despite working in separate physical locations, technology can give you numerous opportunities for seamless, recurring communication—allowing the people you coach to document their progress and giving you extra touch-points to demonstrate your support.

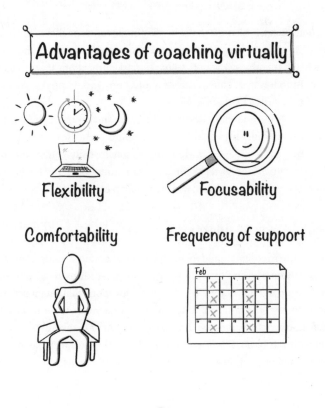

Advantages of coaching virtually

Flexibility

Focusability

Comfortability

Frequency of support

# THE DISADVANTAGES OF COACHING VIRTUALLY

Like anything else, virtual coaching also has its drawbacks. But if you're aware of the potential obstacles, you'll be better prepared to overcome them and make the most of the virtual coaching experience.

## Difficulties Building Rapport and Trust

Virtual teams don't meet in the breakroom at lunch or chat in the hallways, so leaders miss out on casual, spontaneous engagement with their staff members. The natural bonds and connections that typically form from frequent conversations about non-work-related topics are lost in the virtual world of work.

If you have already developed a relationship through face-to-face contact with the person you are coaching, there's less of a gap. But coaching someone online when you've never really gotten to know them in person can be a challenge. It's not impossible, but it will take more time and effort, served with a big scoop of patience.

## Technology Problems

Spotty internet signals and frozen images can certainly undermine the momentum of your discussions. The same goes for poor lighting and bad sound quality. Then factor in all the questions that might be running through the minds of the people you coach: *Is the camera at the right angle, or is my boss looking up my nose? Am I speaking too loudly? Does my background look cluttered?* While being comfortable in your home is great, it could also come with lots of unknowns.

## New Distractions

While traditional office distractions are eliminated when people work from home, completely different distractions can happen during your coaching sessions. If you're coaching on your laptop, notifications may pop up that weren't there when all of your devices were put away, as recommended in Chapter 3. Then fold in the natural distractions that come with working in the home environment like barking dogs, small children needing help, delivery drivers ringing the doorbell, and noisy lawn mowers passing by the window. There's simply no way to eliminate some of these elements when working remotely.

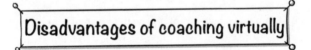

**Disadvantages of coaching virtually**

**Difficulties building rapport**

**New distractions**

**Technology problems**

# GUIDELINES FOR VIRTUAL COACHING

Virtual coaching is here to stay, so you'll need to choose whether you want to lean into the advantages or feel frustrated by its limitations. Managers who want to expand their impact and influence must shift their thinking and accept that coaching virtually is a skill that needs to be a permanent part of their leadership toolbox. The guidelines that follow will help you adopt the best practices to take on this essential competency.

## Before Your Coaching Sessions

The environment you create among the members of your team plays a significant role in virtual coaching sessions, just as it does with the in-person version. While it might seem more casual to connect through a screen, preparation is still vitally important. Make sure you invest the same time and energy you would for a face-to-face meeting.

### *Prioritize Relationship-Building*

Be deliberate about finding opportunities to develop relationships with your team members, preferably before you launch into virtual coaching. This could mean trying to be in the office the same day as your coachees or holding regularly scheduling in-person events like lunches, happy hours, or group attendance at an industry conference. The specifics are up to you, but here's the main point: If you have an option to create some face-to-face interactions, make that a priority.

If your team members are located on different continents, in-person gatherings may not be an option, which means you'll simply have to find a way to build relationships virtually. Set aside time at the start of virtual team meetings and coaching sessions for casual conversation before getting down to business. Consider using ice-breakers or games that get your employees engaged on a different level. For instance, send out a fun "prompt" to the team before a virtual meeting like:

Tell us something new you learned this week.

Use an icon that most represents how you feel today.

Share an interesting fact no one knows about you.

Tell us what you most need right now to help you feel productive.

Another great option is establishing virtual office hours where your team members can drop by online to ask a quick question or get your opinion on something. This casual, open-door policy online allows you to create opportunities that mimic the interactions that might happen in the office breakroom or hallway. No appointment needed. And there's always the chance that multiple employees drop by at the same time to increase team communication and maybe even allow for a spontaneous brainstorming session.

*Make Technology Work Seamlessly on Your End*

Unless you have no other choice, coach from your laptop rather than your phone. Initiate the video calls in a place with strong Wi-Fi. Situate your chair so you are a comfortable distance from the camera. If you're sitting too close or the angle isn't optimal, you may look overly dominant or intimidating. If you need to, elevate your laptop using a riser or a stack of books to get the camera at eye level. Test your lighting and sound to be optimal and ensure that your video background looks clean and professional.

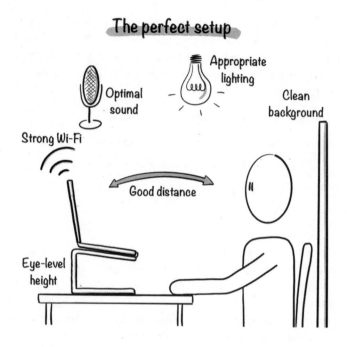

*Be Strategic About the Timing of Your Coaching Sessions*

In a virtual setting, the people you coach get an up-close and constant view of your eyes—which are not only the window to your soul, but a billboard that advertises your energy level and demeanor, too. If you start your workday feeling refreshed and energized, schedule time to coach during the mornings. On the other hand, if you're someone who doesn't hit your stride until midday, save your coaching conversations for the afternoons.

In the same vein, don't jam-pack your schedule so full of meetings that you don't have a few minutes to prepare and establish the right mindset before you start each virtual coaching session. It can be hard to focus on coaching when you're still thinking about the action items you need to tackle from the last two meetings. If your mind is scattered, they'll see it in your eyes.

### Create a Distraction-Free Zone

Shut off your phone and turn off any applications that might fight for your attention during your online coaching, especially email. Move your to-do lists to the far side of the desk and, if there are additional devices in your space that might be competing for bandwidth on your internet connection, adjust accordingly.

If there are other people sharing the office area in your remote location or if you're at home with kids, let your colleagues or family know you will be unavailable for a period of time. Consider putting a sign on the door saying you're unavailable and not to be disturbed while the coaching session is underway.

## During Your Coaching Sessions

Once it's time to begin your virtual meeting, there are some strategies you can use to optimize the quality of your session.

### Leverage Video to Create a More Personal Experience

Don't give in to the temptation to do audio-only coaching. Make sure you and your coachee turn on your cameras so you can gather all of the rich information from seeing someone's face and interpreting their expressions. Use the opening moments of the virtual session to connect on a deeper level, just as you would with an in-person meeting.

Start with some casual conversation before you get down to business:

"What's going on with your family these days?"

"Have you been watching the new crime docuseries on Netflix? Everyone at my house is hooked on that show."

"Are you ready for the upcoming holidays? I haven't even started my shopping."

This is also a good time to follow up on something the person may have shared with you previously:

"The last time we talked, you told me your son was trying to decide between Ohio State and Notre Dame. Did he make a choice yet?"

"I remember you mentioned that your mom had been in the hospital. How is she doing?"

### Set the Parameters for Your Virtual Conversation

Begin your discussion by outlining the purpose or goal and the time frame allotted. You might say something like:

"I've got one hour blocked out, and I'd like to talk about the customer quarterly review meeting we had yesterday. I think there are some opportunities we can take away from that."

"We've got 45 minutes together today, and I want to get your perspective on the project status."

### Follow Good Time Management Practices

Take responsibility for keeping your virtual coaching sessions on track and ending on time. But be aware that this can be a little tricky when you're doing everything you can to maintain eye contact. A great idea is to set a timer and use it to make sure you're progressing through the discussion at an appropriate speed to cover all of your topics. As the leader, it's your job to add this kind of structure to the conversations. For example:

> "Let's put a pin in that subject for now and move on. I want to make sure we have time to talk about the quarterly forecast."

> "Sounds like you have quite a few ideas for the event theme. In the interest of time, which one would you recommend and why?"

> "We only have a few minutes left, but I'd like to hear your action items based on our conversation today."

### *Commit to a World-Class Level of Focus*

In a virtual setting, it's more important than ever to stay mentally plugged in. After all, your coachee will be looking right at you for the duration of your conversation—scanning for context clues from your facial expressions and eye contact (or lack of it). The coachee will detect if your mind has wandered or if you're mindlessly flipping through some papers while he or she is talking.

While that may sound daunting, you should be applying that same heightened level of focus to your listening skills in the virtual environment. Be diligent about hearing the message but also pay close attention to the body language that accompanies it. What's the subtext? It's harder to detect through the computer screen, but be proactive about looking for hints that help you read between the lines. If body language is problematic, you might say something like:

"I know you said we're still on track to meet the deadline, but I think I detected some hesitation. Are there some roadblocks we should discuss?"

"How are things going in terms of the collaboration with the finance department? I can tell you've been picking your words carefully on that subject, which made me wonder if there's an underlying concern."

## Push Yourself to Get Creative with Your Virtual Coaching Techniques

Your conversations don't have to involve the two of you staring at each other's faces on a computer screen for an hour. Think outside the lines. How could you incorporate a whiteboard? What screen-sharing visuals could you integrate as part of your conversation? Could you show a video to demonstrate a particular point? Mix it up. To increase engagement, find some creative ways to add variety to your virtual conversations.

## Be Gracious About Interruptions

Working from a remote location may involve uncontrollable factors that get in the way, even when someone takes every precaution in advance. Maintain a sense of humor and do your best to alleviate any anxiety your coachee might experience because of an unavoidable interruption:

"Things happen. Don't worry about it."

"No problem at all. We can work around that."

## After Your Coaching Sessions

If you want your investment in virtual coaching to pay off, put some measures into place to help you maintain momentum and see things through.

### Follow Up Applies Here Too

Following up might be even more important after a virtual conversation since you miss some of the usual cues that help you evaluate how the conversation went. On video, you get facial expressions, but not the complete picture of the person's body language. Sure, you get visual feedback while the camera is on, but you also lose out on monitoring attitudes in the breakroom later that day. Follow-up questions are extremely critical to make sure your perception of the session and the coachee's match. You could circle back by phone, with an email, or even through a platform like Slack with questions like these:

> "Did you feel like our session was productive on Monday?"

> "Are there any changes you might make to the format of our session for next time?"

• • •

Given the current factors at play in the business world and society in general, it's safe to assume virtual coaching is here to stay. While there are some challenges, the extraordinary benefits of coaching outweigh the hurdles that sometimes come with the online version.

Here's the important thing to remember: By following specific strategies, you can quickly become proficient in the virtual coaching process and eventually produce the same results you'd get in person.

That creates a positive and enriching experience for you and for the people you coach—with the convenience and flexibility of making it happen in a virtual environment.

## ESSENTIAL TAKEAWAYS

- Remember that coaching pays off—even if it has to be done virtually.

- Make virtual coaching a skill set that's a permanent part of your leadership toolbox since remote work is a trend that will continue.

- Prioritize some face-to-face interactions in your coaching relationships if you have that option.

- Always leave time to prepare and establish the right mindset before you start each virtual coaching session.

## PART III

# BEYOND THE ESSENTIALS

CHAPTER

# 10

# Effective Questions

**Great questions are the** key to successful coaching. This chapter includes a range of themes you can incorporate into your own coaching conversations and modify as needed. You'll find a variety of approaches for both Performance and Developmental Coaching. Think about which questions feel most natural for you, based on your personal communication style, and start to weave them into your next coaching session.

## COACHING FRAMEWORK–DRIVEN QUESTIONS

A simple way to think about the questions you use in coaching conversations is to link them directly to the five-step framework in Chapter 2. This will keep you on track to cover all of the critical components needed for an efficient, effective discussion. With that in mind, let's walk through the framework steps so you can determine which questions work best at different points in a coaching session.

## Step 1: Assess the Situation

In Step 1, you'll work to help identify specific problems that need attention, pinpoint performance challenges, uncover career aspirations, or overcome hurdles to advancement. The following questions can be used in your coaching sessions to achieve those goals in assessing the situation:

- What can you tell me about _____?
- What do you think about _____?
- What do you make of _____?
- How do you feel about _____?
- What concerns you the most about _____?
- What impact is this having on you now?
- What impact is this having on the team/company/customers?
- What seems to be your main obstacle?
- What do you mean by _____?
- What else can you tell me about _____?
- What is holding you back from _____?
- What would make an ideal work situation for you?
- What special interests do you have?
- What activities inspire you the most?
- What is your ideal outcome?
- How do you want _____ to turn out?

## Step 2: Generate Ideas

In Step 2, you'll guide coachees to analyze potential solutions for the challenges they have identified. The following questions may help as you work with them to generate ideas:

- What choices/actions would be most likely to help you meet your goal?

- Is there an obvious solution, or does this require something more creative?

- What solutions have you tried?

- What has worked for you already?

- How could you do more of that?

- What hasn't worked so far?

- What did you learn from trying _____?

- What do you think is stopping you from trying _____?

- What could you change about your approach to get a better result?

- What could you have done differently?

- How might you handle it next time?

- What skills/experiences do you think might make you more effective/promotable?

- How could you demonstrate your leadership ability, even if you're not technically a leader?

- Are there ways to gain some of the experiences you need outside of your current role (industry organization involvement, community service, committee leadership)?

## Step 3: Develop an Action Plan

In Step 3, you'll prompt coachees to strategically filter through the ideas generated, determine the best solution, gain clarity on the specific steps needed to implement that solution, and prepare for any hurdles along the way. By guiding them to link their action items to results, you strengthen their decision-making skills and improve their confidence. The following questions can support your goals in these conversations:

- What solution do you propose? And why?

- What are the downsides, if any?

- What obstacles could get in the way of success?

- How can you overcome those obstacles?

- If you do this, how will it affect _____?

- What is the cost of *not* doing this?

- What else do you need to consider?

- What is your overall plan to implement this solution?

- What are your next steps?

- How will you know when you have succeeded?

## Step 4: Provide Support

In Step 4, you'll keep the accountability for outcomes fully on the people you are coaching while offering to use your knowledge, network, and clout to expedite their success. The following questions can provide the structure for those pivotal discussions:

- How can I support you in making this happen?

- What do you need to begin the process?

- What else might be helpful to know as you pursue this?

- Who else can support you as you take on this project?

- Are there any connections I can facilitate to speed up the process?

- Are there any obstacles you anticipate that I might be able to remove?

- What would make you more comfortable with taking this on?

- Would you like me to look at the report/presentation before you submit it?

## Step 5: Follow Up

In Step 5, you'll work to stay connected and assess the progress of the people you're coaching, evaluate their strategic thinking, determine whether they are implementing the action plan you've developed together, and identify any bumps in the road. These follow-up questions may be helpful in making your analysis:

- How are things going with your project/experiment?

- What did you take away from the book/podcast I recommended?

- What was the best thing you learned in the training class?

- How did the informational interview go?

- How do you feel about the progress you are making so far toward your goal?

- What shifts have you seen in how you are handling _____?

- What reactions have you noticed from your colleagues/clients since you changed _____?

- Have any of the original variables shifted?

- Have you uncovered anything that might make you rethink your goal or strategy?

● ● ●

It's impossible to overstate the value of great questions in a coaching conversation. On the surface, those questions gather important information. But the real genius behind them is how they can prompt your coachees to think about situations in a whole new way: shifting into strategic mode, stretching their creative muscles, looking for the not-so-obvious options, and solving problems on their own. If you can learn to ask brilliant questions at the right times, you can become the coach within your organization that employees are clamoring to work with.

## ESSENTIAL TAKEAWAYS

- Great questions are the key to successful coaching.

- When you align your questions with each step in your coaching framework, you can stay on track to cover all of the critical components needed for an efficient, effective discussion.

- By guiding coachees to link their action items to results, you help them strengthen their decision-making skills and improve their confidence.

# Coaching for Cognitive and Cultural Diversity

**We've talked throughout this** book about the need for coaches to put themselves in the shoes of the people they are coaching. Admittedly, that can be challenging, in any situation. But what happens if the person you're coaching has experienced the world in a very different way than you?

So many aspects of our lives play a role in who we are as individuals and shape the way we think—and these aspects can include race, age, gender, sexual orientation, religion, culture, environments, backgrounds, and more. Part of inclusion is making others feel that their thoughts, experiences, values, and morals are heard and accepted, even if they are different from yours. Inclusion involves accepting that diversity of thought, and when it comes to coaching, it also involves making others feel that their thoughts, experiences, and values are heard and respected. The reality is you could be in a coaching situation where you and your coachee arrive at the table with two very different approaches when it comes to thinking, processing information, or seeing the world.

As you'll recall, Chapter 4 highlighted the requirements for coaches to be emotionally intelligent (sensitive to the needs of their coachees), impartial and fair (setting aside any bias or assumptions you might have), insatiably curious (working to understand other perspectives and find value in those), kind and considerate (making coachees feel comfortable and providing them with a safe space to be vulnerable), and genuinely affirming (recognizing and respecting the unique skills and talents your coachees bring to the discussion). In an inclusive coaching situation, the importance of these characteristics is magnified many times over.

Consider this: The coaching relationship provides a perfect platform for two people with diverse backgrounds to connect on a meaningful level and invest the time to understand their different or even opposing viewpoints. From that perspective, I bet you can see why I believe that inclusive coaching provides one of the greatest opportunities to "walk a mile in someone else's shoes" and to learn from each other.

## BENEFITS OF INCLUSIVE COACHING

When we combine the proven results of coaching with the incredible and proven advantages of more inclusive workplaces, we discover a winning strategy with benefits for everyone involved. Let's look at these benefits a bit more:

**For coachees:** No matter your coachees' individual profile or thinking, coaching can help them accelerate their careers. But that benefit is even more critical for people who may have been previously overlooked or excluded because of a difference in background or their thinking. Coaching can become a gateway to help them feel more valued and included in the workplace, which is typically linked to a better sense of well-being along with higher job satisfaction, engagement, performance, motivation, and creativity.

**For you, as a coach:** Developing an ongoing relationship with someone whose background and life experiences look nothing like yours can help expand your worldview. You get a unique opportunity to learn and grow as a leader, as well as a human being. The process may also allow you to uncover any unconscious areas of bias and begin working to eliminate those.

**For organizations:** Besides reducing turnover rates, inclusive coaching allows companies to make a strong statement about their commitment to developing and supporting those who may have been unheard, underrepresented, or marginalized in the past. It offers organizations a tangible way to support diversity and inclusion efforts. More specifically, it allows them to invest in a multifaceted employee population that can contribute greater diversity of thought, increase innovation, and positively impact their companies' success.

## GUIDELINES FOR BECOMING AN INCLUSIVE COACH

For starters, all the general strategies for coaching recommended in this book apply here. However, some apply more directly within the context of being a more inclusive coach.

## Respect Individual Differences in Your Coachees

We all develop skills or make progress at a different pace. With that in mind, be flexible about meeting your coachees wherever they are, rather than assuming they will follow the same patterns you did along your development journey.

Another area of contrast may emerge as you work to set challenging yet realistic goals for diverse coachees. Keep in mind that everyone has different career aspirations and your coachees' goals may not be what you would expect. Be careful not to superimpose *your* expectations on *their* career preferences or the way they achieve outcomes.

### *Focus on Cognitive Diversity*

Conformity of thought breeds stagnation and can imperil the long-term success of organizations, so your focus should instead be on tapping into *cognitive diversity*. Initiatives that support and seek out diversity of thought deserve a place alongside programs that build demographic diversity.

As you coach team members, focus on helping them make it a habit to see things from a different perspective and consistently push their creative boundaries. That's a great way to start folding cognitive diversity into everything your team does.

## *Be Patient with the Process*

If you're having trouble relating to anyone you coach, for whatever reason, building rapport with that person may take longer and be more challenging. Remember that those who have experienced discrimination (whether that's a result of their cultures, backgrounds, or beyond) may be more reluctant to open up and achieve a level of trust with a coach. Take the time to find something you have in common and build on that.

Be patient as you work to develop relationships with your coachees. Let them know that you are genuinely interested in their perspectives and that you value their contributions, even if the way they reach their conclusions doesn't sync with your approach. When you are consistent about coaching with that level of respect and openness, you will soon prove that you're a worthy, compassionate partner.

## *Lead with Humility*

Deliberately set your ego aside when thinking about opposing beliefs, different cultures, and varying capacities to take in and process information. It's tempting to think that your background, experience, and know-how give you the natural edge on producing the best ideas and solutions. Recognize that tendency and override it in your brain.

When coaching from a place of humility, you display a true willingness to learn from others and temporarily take your opinion out of the equation. What happens when you do that? You may discover a superior solution or an option you'd never considered before.

## Share Your Rationale

When we know someone well (a spouse, sibling, best friend), we sometimes feel comfortable speaking in shorthand because our spheres of experience have a significant overlap. They seem to instinctively know what we're thinking or what we mean, even if we don't communicate it in specific terms.

When you are coaching, you can't rely on that same comprehension overlap. Consequently, it's imperative to have a greater sense of transparency about what you are doing, why you are doing it, and how you came to those decisions. If you neglect to share your thinking and rationale during your coaching conversations, the probability of misunderstandings is exponentially higher.

The lesson there? Make it a priority to clarify your thought processes with your coachees. Don't assume that they don't care or won't understand your thinking. Thoroughly explaining your rationale will help you become a more effective coach and avoid causing any unnecessary anxiety or concern on the part of your employees.

## Express Your Willingness to Discuss Difficult Topics

During coaching conversations, the diverse people you coach may want to talk about their differences and the impact those might be having on them in the workplace—with colleagues, customers, or vendors. Those conversations may be uncomfortable. But it's incredibly important as a coach to let your employees know you are willing to talk about anything affecting their performance, their potential career growth, and, most importantly, their well-being at work.

Remember you aren't expected to have all the answers, particularly when it comes to experiences you can't fully understand. This is definitely the time to lead with empathy, patience, kindness, and compassion. And if you decide you're in over your head, be honest about that. Loop in someone from human resources or a person who has been trained in facilitating difficult conversations. While you may not be able to solve the problem, your willingness to talk about it goes a long way toward strengthening your coaching relationships.

## Promote Talent from Different Backgrounds

An article in *Forbes* (March 3, 2022) by business leader Desmund Adams cites research indicating that "diverse workforces are twice as likely to meet or exceed their financial goals." Adams adds that recruiting for diversity can also increase net income (earnings) by 33 percent. Those certainly aren't insignificant numbers! He explains the direct connection in this way: "Diversity drives innovation; innovation drives profitability."[*]

As a coach, you're in a unique position to help your organization tap into those bottom-line advantages when you support and promote people from different backgrounds. Your coaching efforts can elevate the physical, cultural, and cognitive diversity in your company to help create a competitive advantage in the marketplace.

● ● ●

While the company benefits are convincing enough to prioritize inclusive coaching, far more important is the fact that you will be making everyone on your team feel they are valuable. And, you will create an environment where people feel heard, respected, and safe being who they are.

By coaching and supporting people with different backgrounds and thought patterns, you can help create an environment where

---

[*] Desmund Adams, "How to Start Treating Human Resources as the Engine of Profit," *Forbes*, 2022, https://www.forbes.com/sites/forbesbusinesscouncil/people/desmundadams/?sh=4a11afb2482e.

people feel they can bring their whole selves to work—while also generating impressive benefits for leaders, employees, and the organizations they serve.

## ESSENTIAL TAKEAWAYS

- The coaching relationship provides a perfect platform for two people with diverse backgrounds to connect on a meaningful level and invest the time to understand their different or even opposing viewpoints.

- Inclusive coaching comes with benefits for everyone: coachees, coaches, and the companies they work for.

- Conformity of thought breeds stagnation and can imperil the long-term success of organizations, so your focus should be on tapping into cognitive diversity.

- If you neglect to share your thinking and rationale during your coaching conversations, the probability of misunderstandings is exponentially greater.

**CHAPTER**

# 12

# Powerful Phrases

**Starting, continuing, and ending** coaching sessions all come with their own challenges. In this chapter, you'll be armed with ready-to-use dialogue that will help pave the way for more effective coaching sessions or allow you to pivot mid-conversation and address important issues. Expect to refer to this chapter frequently in your coaching journey.

## GETTING STARTED

Sometimes the hardest part of coaching is getting started and setting the right tone for a conversation—especially conversations that involve confronting a problem. I've heard this feedback from leaders at every level for many years. They say things like: "I feel more confident about coaching once the discussion is under way. But I do tend to fumble for words at the beginning, and it seems kind of awkward."

If that statement resonates with you (as it does for many), these phrases will help:

**"I'd love to hear the details about how things went with the quarterly customer review."**

> This statement invites the coachee to share key facts and a personal evaluation of the event, which will provide valuable input to guide the coaching conversation.

**"Let's discuss how you might begin to take better advantage of one of your real strengths."**

> This statement demonstrates a sense of partnership by acknowledging the coachee's skills and talents, while engaging the person in a conversation about how to leverage those qualities for career advancement.

**"I'm not sure we got the response we were hoping for with the presentation yesterday. May I share with you what I observed?"**

> This statement communicates a shared concern about the outcome of the event without placing blame or making the coachee feel defensive before the conversation even begins. Asking permission before expressing those thoughts creates a more cordial environment for the discussion.

**"I noticed in the meeting that you seemed to dismiss Bill whenever he made some suggestions. Was that your intent?"**

> This statement expresses an observation in a more direct way, while the question gives the coachee the benefit of the doubt and an opportunity to confirm or correct the initial impression.

**"This may not be what you were hoping to hear today. But I'm sharing this with you because I know you want to grow in this position and potentially advance."**

This statement acknowledges the coachee's potential disappointment about a decision or event while reinforcing the partnership to make improvements that will allow the person to keep moving forward to meet his or her goals.

## MOVING THE CONVERSATION ALONG

At some point in your coaching discussion, you may discover the conversation has stalled or gotten off track. A well-timed question can help you reset and refocus. In many cases, you can pair an observation you've made with a request to provide some of your own insights. The following questions do exactly that and may be helpful to move conversations forward:

**"Those are some good ideas. Would you be interested in hearing a few of mine?"**
> This statement affirms the creative thinking of the coachee, while the follow-up question politely opens the door to expand or shift the thought process for greater impact.

**"Perhaps something is getting in the way of you showing up as your best self. Are you open to hearing what I think might be keeping you from being at your best?"**
> This statement shows you recognize your coachee's untapped potential and want to help the person overcome obstacles impeding success.

**"You mentioned you're skeptical about getting together one-on-one with Marci. What conditions would make you more comfortable with that step?"**

> This statement acknowledges your coachee's concerns and respectfully works to explore alternatives that will lead to positive outcomes.

**"I can tell you are disappointed with that outcome. In retrospect, what could you have done differently?"**

> This statement allows you to empathetically recognize the employee's feelings, while helping the coachee rethink the strategies and approaches used in a less-than-successful effort.

**"I understand your perspective here. I see it differently. May I tell you why?"**

> This statement demonstrates that you have been listening *and* understand the employee's point of view. Politely offering to share a different perspective may shed new light on the situation, too.

## WRAPPING UP

Great coaching conversations often cover a lot of different topics. One way to help your coachees digest all of that information is by asking targeted questions that help them summarize and recap. As you guide the conversation to an end, highlight any items that might have been overlooked or discuss potential obstacles that could impede their next steps. For example:

**"Before we move on, is there anything I've missed? Anything I haven't taken into account?"**

> These questions are cleverly stated in reference to the coach but put the responsibility on employees to think through the details and logistics on a more granular level.

**"So it sounds like you don't feel comfortable adding that to your development plan. Is there something else that you'd be willing to try?"**

> This statement conveys understanding that the employee has concerns about tackling certain action items but gives him or her the flexibility to suggest alternatives.

**"Given our conversation today, are you prepared to launch the project? And if not, what do you need to feel more confident about that?"**

> This statement allows your coachee to express any concerns about moving forward and identify areas that will likely require your ongoing support.

**"I know it has been a tough year. How do you think this experience has prepared you for the future or given you the tools to be more resilient?"**

> This statement acknowledges the challenges that might be weighing down the employee and prompts the person to think about the long-term career advantages of the lessons learned during difficult times.

**"Was today's conversation valuable for you? Is there anything you wish could have been different?"**

This statement demonstrates that you really are invested in making a difference for your coachee, and you value the employee's feedback as part of your coaching relationship.

• • •

Experienced coaches know the importance of using powerful phrases to guide their conversations. If you're armed with dialogue starters and phrases that help you move through each phase of the coaching process, you can feel more comfortable with the process and ultimately elevate your impact as a coach.

## ESSENTIAL TAKEAWAYS

- Powerful phrases can serve as tools that help you pivot mid-conversation to address important issues.

- Sometimes the hardest part of coaching is getting started and setting the right tone for a conversation—especially conversations that involve confronting a problem.

- If a conversation has stalled or gotten off track, a well-timed question can help you reset and refocus.

- One way to help your coachees digest all of the information covered in a coaching session is by asking targeted questions that help them summarize and recap.

CHAPTER

13

# The Ongoing Journey of Coaching

**As you apply your** coaching skills in real-life situations, it's essential to keep this in mind: Becoming a world-class coach requires practice and takes time. It won't happen overnight. And the truth is, it's a continuous learning process. Every employee you coach will be different, and maybe that's why so many leaders love the challenge.

As we wrap up, let's treat this like a coaching session and develop an action plan. What are your next steps? How can you take what you've learned here and put it into action?

One of the first things you can do is think about coaching as something that's woven into your role as a leader every day, rather than something you do on, say, Tuesday mornings. With this in mind, what current situations offer a great chance to start using your coaching skills? Don't wait for a closed-door meeting with your coachees to talk about their career goals and motivation. Every chance you get, acknowledge that you have their backs and are rooting for them to succeed and advance. When that attitude is pervasive throughout your conversations, your formal coaching sessions will feel much more natural.

If you are feeling hesitant about diving in headfirst, dip your toe in the coaching pool by doing some role-play exercises with a trusted colleague or friend. Ask this person to play the part of someone on your team and provide basic background information without adding any opinions or judgments. Then dive right in! Start your mini-coaching session and allow the person to play along, responding in any way he or she wants. This gives you a great opportunity to test the impact of your approach and delivery. Since you won't have any idea what the other person is going to say, you'll also get to practice your in-the-moment reactions and determine if you are ready to handle whatever curveballs are thrown in your direction by your actual coachees.

If you already had some experience coaching, this is a great time to reach out to former or current employees for their feedback on your process up until now. Share with them that you are taking steps to "up your game" when it comes to coaching, and that you could benefit from their perspectives about your strengths and any areas for improvement. Select those who will give you candid and constructive input, and be sure to keep an open mind as you hear their comments.

A great way to maintain your enthusiasm for learning this important competency is to monitor your progress along the journey. You've already completed the benchmark assessment once, and I encourage you to repeat this assessment at six-month intervals and track your changes in the Progress Tracker chart that follows. This will help you pinpoint the areas with the most impressive growth, as well as identify opportunities for further development.

Go ahead and set a reminder in your calendar now to take this assessment six months from today. Then, do the same for 12, 18, and 24 months from now as well.

# Coaching Self-Assessment

**Directions:** Please read each statement below and use the following scale to indicate how strongly you agree with it. Then add up the rating column for a total score at the bottom.

1 = Never
2 = Rarely
3 = Sometimes
4 = Usually
5 = Always

| Rating | |
|---|---|
| | When coaching employees, I assume positive intent. |
| | I keep an open mind and try to understand the point of view of others. |
| | When coaching employees, I show genuine curiosity in what they have to say. |
| | I ask probing and open-ended questions to better understand a situation before giving my advice. |
| | When I listen, I try to clarify what my employees have said by summarizing what I heard. |
| | When listening, I give my full attention and put all distractions aside. |
| | I demonstrate attentiveness with eye contact and body language. |

| | |
|---|---|
| | I provide positive and negative feedback in a timely manner. |
| | I help employees recognize their strengths and areas for improvement. |
| | I help employees understand the impact of their behavior. |
| | I help employees identify any potential misalignment between their intended impact and how others actually experience them. |
| | I give my employees the benefit of the doubt. |
| | I take time to understand the long-term career aspirations of the people I coach. |
| | I encourage my employees to challenge their own assumptions and explore new ideas/approaches. |
| | I help employees come up with their own solutions rather than imposing mine. |
| | I support my employees in identifying goals that will have the most impact on their success at work. |
| | I partner with my employees to create development plans that will help them become more effective in reaching their immediate goals. |
| | I partner with my employees to create development plans targeted to prepare them for career advancement. |
| | I believe that I genuinely share in the success of those I coach. |

| | | |
|---|---|---|
| | I offer continuous support, encouragement, and accountability as part of my coaching practice. | |
| | **Maximum Score: 100** | |

| Progress Tracker | | |
|---|---|---|
| | **Date Taken** | **Score** |
| **Original Benchmark** | | |
| **6-Month Assessment** | | |
| **12-Month Assessment** | | |
| **18-Month Assessment** | | |
| **24-Month Assessment** | | |

If you follow the strategies in this book and practice regularly, I'm confident you'll see impressive results in your assessment scores and, more importantly, in the people you are coaching.

When I think about my work as a leadership consultant, I can honestly say that coaching has been one of the most rewarding parts of my business. The fact that research overwhelming proves its value—for the individuals involved, as well as the organization—is just a bonus.

I always consider it a privilege to support others in their career development, and watching their growth is extremely satisfying. It never gets old—and I wish nothing but the same for you. As you embark on your own journey as a coach, I hope you will find as much joy in the process as I always have and still do.

Wishing you all the best,

Sara

# Coaching
# Essentials Toolkit

**To help maximize the** knowledge you gained from this book, I want to provide some resources that support your growth as a coach. The components in this section include the following:

- The Dos and Don'ts of Coaching

- Coaching Framework Guide

- Coaching Preparation Worksheet

- Coaching Development Plan

- Coaching Development Plan Template

# THE DOS AND DON'TS OF COACHING

## Dos

- Build trust and nurture strong relationships with your coachees

- Position yourself as a partner in their success

- Be fully present

- Set the intention up front

- Confirm confidentiality—and keep that promise

- Maintain clarity about your role and your purpose as a coach

- Use a framework as your guide

- Ask open-ended questions

- Suspend judgment

- Finish with an action plan

- Hold them accountable for their commitments

## Don'ts

- Confuse the role of coaching with training, counseling, or discipline related to poor performance

- Rely only on your coachees to identify their needs

- Fail to set ambitious goals that align with your coachees' strengths, motivations, and interests

- Talk in code ("you need to be more strategic") rather than translating your recommendations into actionable steps with examples

- Neglect to enhance your own self-awareness and emotional intelligence

- Assume you wouldn't benefit from insights and feedback provided by your own coach or mentor

- Underestimate the potential of your direct reports

- Underestimate your own potential as a successful coach

# COACHING FRAMEWORK GUIDE

The information that follows provides a high-level summary of the coaching framework from Chapter 2. This at-a-glance resource may add value as you prepare for coaching conversations. It can also help keep you on track as you cover each of the five steps found within the framework.

## Step 1: Assess the Situation

- Clarify the session purpose *(Development, Performance, Support)*

- Remain neutral

- Start the conversation *(Lead with facts/observations or ask for their perspective)*

- Use open-ended questions to prompt richer discussions

- Examples:

  "In the meeting, I noticed that . . . "

  "How do you think the presentation went?"

  "May I share what I observed . . . ?"

## Step 2: Generate Ideas

- Ask for suggestions and alternatives

- Listen actively without judgment

- Use prompts to stretch their thinking *(What if)*

- Discuss the pros and cons

- Examples:

  "Based on the facts we know right now, what alternatives have you considered?"

  "What if the parameters change next quarter?"

  "Are there any downsides to that strategy?"

  "What skills could give you an edge in this situation and move you closer to your goal of advancement?"

## Step 3: Develop an Action Plan

- Set goals to achieve the desired results

- Establish a strategy

- Determine short- and long-term deliverables and deadlines

- Define tools for measurement

- Get agreement before moving forward

- Examples:

  "What's the ideal outcome for this?"

  "What steps would you need to take to make that happen?"

"It sounds like you are interested in expanding your capacity in that area. What type of development would be most helpful for you?"

## Step 4: Provide Support

- Offer your time

- Share your knowledge

- Give access to key resources

- Connect them with others who can add value

- Remove any obstacles that are blocking their success

- Examples:

    "How can I support you?"

    "I'd like to introduce you to one of my contacts. She can give you a wealth of information about this subject."

    "Is there anything getting in the way of meeting your goals?"

## Step 5: Follow Up

- Schedule regular check-in meetings

- Monitor progress

- Course-correct if needed

- Examples:

"Tell me how things are going with your progress."

"Have you encountered anything that made you rethink your current strategy?"

"If that approach isn't working, what other strategy could give you better traction?"

"What have you learned from working on this? Any big takeaways?"

"How has this experience prepared you to take on more responsibility?"

# COACHING PREPARATION WORKSHEET

Taking a more strategic approach to your coaching sessions can help you stay organized, and this worksheet may be helpful as a guide for your conversations. You'll have an automatic prompt to ensure that you cover all the components in the coaching framework, along with space to record your observations and items for follow up.

### Coaching Preparation Worksheet

| Steps | Comments and Observations |
|---|---|
| 1. **Assess the Situation**<br>State the situation and its impact.<br>Get the employee's point of view.<br>Use questions to ensure understanding.<br>Get agreement before moving forward. | |
| 2. **Generate Ideas**<br>Ask the coachee for suggestions first.<br>Listen actively without judging each one individually.<br>Discuss the suggestions and add your own where appropriate. | |
| 3. **Establish an Action Plan**<br>Let the coachee propose an action plan based on the discussion or cocreate next steps based on ideas generated jointly.<br>Support the coachee in achieving his/her action plan. | |

| Steps | Comments and Observations |
|---|---|
| **4. Provide Support**<br>Offer continuous encouragement.<br>Provide resources to support growth.<br>Open doors and remove obstacles. | |
| **5. Follow Up**<br>Set a time and place to follow up with the coachee.<br>Agree to periodic check-ins and updates.<br>Be open to goal or action plan shifts as conditions change. | |

# COACHING DEVELOPMENT PLAN

As leader-coaches, we expect our team members to make action plans and commit to taking deliberate steps to fuel their development. Real growth requires intentionality. So, what about you as a coach? If you want to give focus and direction to your development as an effective coach, you'll want to follow your great advice. Get strategic about your growth!

To help you stay on track, I'm providing the template for a Coaching Development Plan. While there's not a single "right" way to go about the process, most leaders benefit from taking a structured approach that can still be molded to your unique development journey.

Before you start populating the plan, spend some time thinking through your answers to the questions below and considering your options:

- What skills do I need to acquire to become an effective coach?

- Which existing skills do I most want to improve?

- Is there anything I need to stop doing because it is undermining my effectiveness?

- What improvements or changes would deliver the greatest benefit for the people I coach? (Examples include improve listening skills, use more open-ended questions, increase focus, make coaching more of a priority, etc.)

- How can I build accountability into the process so that my growth as a coach becomes an effort in continuous improvement?

- Who can be my role model or mentor to help me sharpen my skills?

- Who can help me practice my coaching skills?

- When can I set aside time regularly to practice my coaching skills?

- Whom can I ask for feedback about my impact as a coach?

- How can I increase the quality of the feedback I receive on my coaching?

- How can I build my self-confidence as a coach?

- When am I at my most/least effective as a coach?

- How will I know I'm making progress?

- How will I know I've achieved my goals so I can set new ones?

Once you've worked through these questions, use the insights you've gained to populate the Coaching Development Plan that follows. If you have multiple goals, action steps, or strategies, list them in priority order to help organize your efforts. Wherever possible, add in deadlines or time parameters to keep your growth process moving forward.

# COACHING DEVELOPMENT PLAN TEMPLATE

**Goals**

*What would I like to achieve as a coach?*

**Action Steps**

*What will I do to work toward those goals?*

**Accountability Strategies**

*How can I sustain focus on my development?*

**Accountability Partners/Mentors**

*Who can help me along the journey?*

**Practice Sessions**

*When will I set aside time to sharpen my coaching skills?*

**Feedback**

*Who could provide me with honest insights
about my coaching abilities?*

**Measurements**

*How will I know when I have achieved my goals?*

# Answer Key for
# Chapter 5 Knowledge Check

1. (d) All of the above
   Leadership coaching has proven benefits for the person being coached, the leader, and the company.
2. A leader's primary role is to develop and inspire high-performing teams, so effective coaching plays a pivotal role in achieving success.
3. The two main types of coaching include Performance Coaching and Developmental Coaching.
4. The five steps in the coaching framework include:
   a. Assess the situation
   b. Generate ideas
   c. Develop an action plan
   d. Provide support
   e. Follow up
5. Types of coaching support include:
   a. Offering continuous encouragement
   b. Providing resources to support growth
   c. Opening doors and removing obstacles
   d. Communicating regularly
6. Building trust and developing rapport are critical first steps in coaching because those qualities form the foundation for relationships that allow for maximum growth and development in the coachees.

7. Open-ended questions are b, d, and f.
8. Listening skills you can use with your coachees include:
    a. Adjusting your frame of mind
    b. Deliberately staying focused
    c. Demonstrating active listening
    d. Paying attention to find any disconnects
    e. Summarizing and paraphrasing
9. Failing to suspend judgment or assume positive intent during coaching creates a negative backdrop for all of your conversations and interactions, which undermines the goal of supporting your employees' growth and development.
10. Great coaches give feedback that is:
    a. Specific
    b. Timely
    c. Purposeful
    d. Tactful
    e. Ongoing
11. Attributes of great coaches include:
    a. Emotionally intelligent
    b. Fully present
    c. Impartial and fair
    d. Insatiably curious
    e. Insightful and perceptive
    f. Genuinely affirming
    g. Patient and composed
    h. Kind and considerate
    i. Growth minded
12. This response and the response to question 13 are unique and personal to you.

# Index

# About the Author

 **Leadership strategist, keynote speaker,** LinkedIn Learning instructor, and award-winning author Sara Canaday is a rare blend of analytical entrepreneur and perceptive warmth. That powerful combination has increasingly made her a go-to resource for helping leaders and high-potential professionals achieve their best.

Her insights come from her real-world experience and a surprising phenomenon she noticed in her own rise up the corporate ladder: The most successful people aren't necessarily the ones with the highest IQs or best job skills. Career advancement is actually more closely linked with how people apply their knowledge and talents—their capacity to collaborate, communicate, and influence others.

Though Sara quickly ascended through the ranks to an executive position in operations with a major company, she realized that helping others maximize their career potential was truly her life's work. After launching her own business as a speaker and consultant, she shared her wisdom through two popular leadership books. The first one,

*You—According to Them: Uncovering the Blind Spots That Impact Your Reputation and Your Career*, established Sara's expertise in leadership development. Her most recent book, *Leadership Unchained: Defy Conventional Wisdom for Breakthrough Performance*, was recognized as a Gold Award Winner by the Nonfiction Authors Association.

Today, Sara is a sought-after leadership speaker and educator, serving diverse organizations around the world. In that capacity, she has gained a unique, frontline view of leadership and its fascinating evolution.

Sara lives in Austin, Texas, with her husband, Brandon; her daughter, Taylor; and her son, Cole.

To stay connected with Sara, go to:

Website: www.SaraCanaday.com

Email: Sara@SaraCanaday.com

LinkedIn: linkedin.com/in/saracanaday/

Twitter: @saracanaday

To sign up for Sara's regular newsletter, please visit her website: www.SaraCanaday.com.

## MORE FROM SARA

Sara shares her targeted content about leadership to diverse audiences around the globe through a wide range of formats: live/virtual keynotes and workshops, video webinars, fireside chats, online education courses with LinkedIn Learning, and her award-winning books.

### *Leadership Unchained: Defy Conventional Wisdom for Breakthrough Performance*

The traditional wisdom that molded leadership for years is losing its effectiveness in our chaotic, digitally overwhelmed world. In some cases, those principles you've always relied on may even impede your progress. Truth is, you can't possibly seize unexpected opportunities or take full advantage of today's innovations if you're stuck using old patterns.

In *Leadership Unchained*, Sara Canaday offers a unique perspective that helps modern leaders break free from the chains of conventional wisdom and blaze new trails toward even greater success.

### *You—According to Them: Uncovering the Blind Spots That Impact Your Reputation and Your Career*

Sara Canaday shares her unique insights on managing workplace reputations in this fascinating book, packed with real case studies and instantly usable strategies. Learn the secrets of accelerating your journey toward success by better understanding yourself and how others perceive you. In *You—According to Them*, Sara offers practical steps to help you leverage the perceptions of a great reputation into bottom-line success.

**McGraw Hill's NEW Business Essentials Series delivers must-know info and action steps for topics every business professional needs to succeed in today's new world of work**

Filled with colored illustrations, assessments, toolkits, action steps, and more, readers will walk away from each book in the Business Essentials Series feeling fully prepared to put their sharpened skills into action right away, even if they never received formal training in that area before!

Organized in three easy-to-digest sections—The Essentials, The Essentials Applied, and Beyond the Essentials—each title in the series shows readers how they can excel in different areas of business from leadership and coaching, all the way to presenting and communicating—in person, online, or a combination of the two.